TELOS

Volume 2

Messages for the Enlightenment of a Humanity in Transition

Aurelia Louise Jones

Mount Shasta Light Publishing

TELOS - Volume 2
Messages for the Enlightenment
of a Humanity in Transformation

ISBN 978-0-9700902-5-6

English Publication - June 2004
Second Printing - April 2006
Third Printing - April 2008
Fourth Printing - January 2010

Mount Shasta Light Publishing
PO Box 1509
Mount Shasta CA 96067-1509 – USA

Phone: 530-926-4599
Fax: 530-926-4159

E-mail: aurelia@mslpublishing.com
Web Site: www.mslpublishing.com
Also: www.lemurianconnection.com

Cover Photography: Erich Ziller
Cover Design: Aaron Rose
Page Layout and Formatting: Aaron Rose

We, as masters of Light, invite you now to choose a more joyful and prosperous destiny for your lives. We urge you to begin creating your lives with much greater ease and grace. The long dark night is now drawing to a close on the surface of our planet, and it is time for all of you to dream a new dream for yourselves and for the Earth.

Let go of all concepts of limitation, sorrow and fear. Believe in the God Presence that beats your heart and create magic in all aspects of your lives. We encourage you to open yourselves fully to all of the wondrous possibilities that await you.

May peace, love, wisdom and deep understanding be your Beacon of Light and may you embrace the consciousness that will bring you back home. We miss you as much as you miss us!

- Adama, Galatia and Ahnahmar

Table of Contents

Part One
Messages from Adama

Part Two
Messages from Various Beings of Telos

Dedication

I dedicate this work to the successful resurgence of the Lemurian consciousness on this planet, a consciousness that came directly from Source Love eons ago. This fifth dimensional awareness was brought to Earth by the beings who formed the Lemurian race. Their love and high level of evolution elevated the Earth into a state of pure bliss and paradise for millions of years. May this resurgence now heal humanity of its perceived separation from the love of its Source.

I dedicate this book to you who are ready and willing to open your hearts to the return of this love, for the Lemurian consciousness and teachings offer the very keys and support you need to bring about personal and planetary evolution.

I also dedicate this work to the Great Lemurian Goddess, to my beloveds, Adama and Ahnahmar, as well as to the High Lemurian Council of Telos from whom I have received so much love and support throughout the ages. I also express my deep appreciation to all those who have been my eternal friends and companions through this long journey of Earth evolution.

Acknowledgements

I wish to express my heartfelt gratitude for the loving support and assistance I have received from many friends world-wide.

In particular, my deepest gratitude goes to all members of the Telos World-Wide Foundation of Montreal, to all members of Telos-France and Telos Europe who work relentlessly for the expansion of the Lemurian mission on our planet.

I also thank all those who are contributing to the expansion of this sacred work in various countries and languages. With deep love and appreciation, I say thank you. Together, one step and one loving action at a time, we are building the foundation to recreate the world we long to experience and to have our beloved Lemurian family among us again.

Preface
Celestia, Sister of Adama

With great admiration and gratitude, we congratulate Aurelia Louise as she presents to you another of her treasured volumes on the history, energy and mission of Lemuria. Aurelia has been a guardian of these energies for lifetimes beyond measure. Her heart's commitment and devotion to her Lemurian family has been unparalleled in the physical realm. Today, she is an emissary unequaled in her desire to share with all humanity the purity of the Lemurian column of love, the Lemurian heart. It is through her heart that we reach out to touch yours.

In this spirit of love and communion that knows no bounds, I invite you to gather with us as you read our words, and connect with the invisible word written between the lines that touch your heart in a personal way. The words of this volume emanate a sacred transmission of awakening. Never before in the history of this planet has such a precious moment so gloriously taken place. We see unfolding wondrous new opportunities for all of you and for all of us in Telos and other Lemurian cities. Your time to remember all that you are is now at hand. It is also time for us to truly celebrate and give gratitude with you for the long awaited "reunion" that is almost upon us.

We offer ourselves toyou as mentors and guides in this awakening. All of us who speak to you from the pages of this book and who visit you in your dreams, meditations and waking hours are here as members of a large family who love you so dearly. We are prepared to support you in whatever form your journey takes.

Each step of your awakening presents an opportunity for joy and understanding that is unsurpassed in your evolution. It opens a door into your own mastery and the opportunity to assist the ever-expanding council of energies that are guiding the Earth through her own awakening.

We send our love to all of you through the joined hands of Adama and Aurelia Louise whose love, thus expressed as an aspect of both realms, may nurture you along your path. We send our remembrances and teachings to you through the wisdom of Adama, Ahnahmar, Angelina and other Elders of Telos and beings of other kingdoms on this planet with whom we work closely. We share our joy with you through the laughter of the children and our visions of what life can be on the surface through the experience and example of our life here in the Earth's interior. We send you blessings from the very center of our souls and from the Heart of our beloved Lemuria.

This lifetime presents to you the greatest mission, the greatest journey of all.

Each time you have incarnated in Lemuria, the Earth's interior or on the surface, you have chosen a mission. You have extended yourself in service to the All. Never before has the goodness that is being created so surpassed the expectations of so many of us. Never before has the spectrum of dimensions blended and created the colors that we are seeing today. Never before has the veil between our world and yours become so thin. Never before has the Love we share and experience with the Divine been so great.

We hold you always in the reservoir of our hearts, joining with you now in the play of pure creation and the dawning of a new world!

(Channeled by Beth Iris, incarnated in Telos as Celestia, sister of Adama)

When you resist what is best
For your pathway,
Your soul will simply allow you
To have your own way
Until you cannot stand it anymore.
We invite you to choose
A more joyful destiny
By making wiser choices for yourself.
- Adama

Introduction and Welcome from Adama

Greetings my dearest brothers and sisters!

It is with great love and renewed friendship that I greet all of you who are about to read Volume 2 of our publications. In Lemuria and Telos we are more than pleased with the overwhelming response and heart openings created by the publication of the first volume. As the patriarch of the vast Lemurian family, I welcome all of you into the embrace of the Lemurian Goddess, the heart of Love and Compassion.

In Telos we knew quite well that, because of their ancient heritage, the French and Spanish populations of this planet would be very receptive to our information. Nevertheless, the amazing response that has manifested everywhere our information has been made available, far surpasses our original expectations. Because of your love and receptivity, we can create and manifest together wondrous positive transformation that will keep unfolding. The wisdom of our teachings will also greatly benefit more of humanity in the years to come and accelerate your evolution.

Many of you are opening your hearts to the memories of your ancient heritage, and becoming willing instruments of a greater acceleration in consciousness on this planet, paving the way for our emergence among you.

We continue to hear so many of you express levels of grief, or sometimes impatience, regarding the time of our emergence. We have noticed the intensity of your yearning for the long awaited reunion. We understand very well what you are going through, and we noticed the tears many of you experienced as you read the first volume. Be assured that as you shed your tears, we supported you with our love and held you in our embrace. Many times we have cried with you, though ours were tears of joy in anticipation of the great reunion to come. Today I ask you to be of good cheer. The precious moment of our emergence has, in fact, already begun. Many of our people from Telos and other Lemurian cities are presently physically living among you, preparing the way for the rest of us.

Because of the high level of unrest and violence still present in your world, those of our surface crew are not yet allowed to identify themselves to you. Several of you have already met some of them physically, but they were always "incognito." A number of our people are living among you now, in several different countries, doing the wondrous work that will ease your future. One day soon, our great light and wisdom will be released into full view for all of you to witness and appreciate. Our channel Aurelia is now aware that she was visited a few months ago in her home by a couple of our "surface crew" incognito. Others of our people have also shown up "physically and undercover" at her public gatherings. This is indeed the beginning of our emergence among you, my friends. Do not despair as it is soon coming! Your period of waiting is almost over; you are now completing the last stage of preparation.

While on this subject, I would like to clarify misunderstandings some hold regarding our emergence. Many of you expect that one day we will come out all at once and find our way to your home to stay with you. This would be quite tricky for all concerned, and not as productive as you might think. Though this could certainly happen in some cases, it would be exceptional. Be also aware that our emergence among you will not take place in a third dimensional vibration. When we emerge, those whose vibration is not raised to a sufficient level will not be able to see us.

Our emergence will be gradual, in accordance with the vibrational shift taking place on the surface and in your environment. We will continue to come out in waves, in small groups, as the people and the planet raise their vibration. Our younger members will be coming first; the elders will come out at a later time. Our present level of emergence has been kept secret and it shall remain that way for a few more years.

We hope that by mid-2006 some of our people will be allowed to contact a few of you in person, having the permission to identify themselves to you. It will be for the purpose of giving you more advanced teachings in small secret gatherings. The criteria for those who will be contacted first remains the same as mentioned in our first volume, and also has to do with the divine plan or mission of each person contacted. Those contacted will have to remain silent about their experiences with us until given permission to share them.

We will first be in touch with those who have dedicated their lives to the service of mankind and consecrated much of their time and finances for the expansion and success of our emergence. Candidates for first contact will be by "invitation only," according to the quality of heart and love/ light frequency maintained on a daily basis by these individuals. Later on, the circle will gradually widen until much of the population will be able to interact with us casually. At all times, only those in resonance with the Lemurian consciousness will be able to see and connect with us.

In the meantime, continue to open yourself to the Divine Heart of Love and Compassion. Study the material we are presenting to you. It contains much wisdom and golden keys to facilitate your spiritual growth and development. Find the areas where the garden of your consciousness needs weeding and fertilizing.

If you read this material only once for the sake of information, it will only serve to expand your bag of knowledge somewhat but will do little for the overall preparation of your ascension into higher consciousness. If you choose to study this material consciously, with an open mind and heart, it will bring much personal transformation into your life. With full intention and determination, you will raise your vibration and then be able to apply these pearls of wisdom into your daily lives. Your efforts will create a flow of positive changes. Much of the material in this book is not so much about information, but about applying the hidden keys contained herein for the ultimate transformation that will lead you to live and walk among us as the masters you are.

I am Adama, your eternal father.

Adama
High Priest of Telos

Part One

Messages from Adama

Within each of you rests a Divine Spark.
Invite it to ignite
The fire of your soul once again.
Encourage it to fuel
The passion of your heart
As you journey home.
- Adama

Chapter One

Dreaming a New Dream for the Planet

Once again, warm greetings from my heart to your heart. It is my pleasure to talk with you once more. The topic you have chosen at this time is dear to my heart. I would like to emphasize how important it is for everyone, especially the lightworkers on this planet, to be consciously creating, in their heart and soul, the vision of the new world in which they want to live and participate. If your heart's desire is to transcend the drudgery of the present-day conditions on the surface and move to an enlightened and blissful way of life, it is now that you have to let go of the old paradigm that has kept you in bondage and pain for so long.

You have all heard the old expression "without vision the people perish." This is so relevant and timely at the cross-roads that humanity and the planet are experiencing at this moment. In Telos and the other subterranean cities, we have kept a vision of the new world on your behalf for a very long time, but understand that we simply cannot do it all for you. By divine law, people living on the surface have to take the responsibility of doing their part. It is time for you to begin consciously dreaming your visions every day, and have them reflected in your aspirations, thoughts, feelings and desires.

At the beginning of the last century, through much determination and dedication, the beloved Master Saint Germain

3

applied to the Godhead and the Galactic Federation of Light for a mighty dispensation. He asked for the "Flame of Freedom" to be released once more on the Earth. After much deliberation and many meetings with various councils of the Godhead, the Galactic Federation of your solar system and several planetary councils, the permission was granted. Freedom is one of the many attributes of the Violet Flame of Transmutation.

> *Without the return of this flame to the surface,*
> *there would be no way for humanity to freely*
> *choose to evolve out of its present state.*

Until that time, the Flame of Freedom, and all of the knowledge and wisdom that comes with it, had been removed from the surface environment for a very long time. This loss of freedom allowed for the limitation you experienced during your many incarnations. The loss of the flame contributed greatly to the suffering experienced by mankind. Because of the karma of the people and the past abuse of this sacred flame, it was withdrawn from the surface at the time of the final sinking of Atlantis.

In your heart, feel the love that Saint Germain has for humanity and open yourself in gratitude for his tireless dedication and service to all of you. In order to secure this dispensation for humanity he had to lay down the energy of his attainment and the pearls of glory of his crown to the Godhead as a security deposit, in the event that humanity misused this flame again. He loved you all so very much that he was willing to take that risk.

> *It remains your job to create the new dream.*
> *What will you create?*

Play your part, dear ones, by actively dreaming a new paradigm for the planet. Envision the type of society you want to live in. Now that the Flame of Freedom has been released, it is your responsibility to create the new world you want to inhabit. Dream your visions of Heaven on Earth and how you would like to see them manifest. Be specific and don't hesitate to include all the wondrous details. You are all co-creator Gods. The Earth is now moving forward into the fifth dimension. A new world is being created but is not yet fully structured or totally defined. It is awaiting your creative contribution.

Everyone will have a slightly different perception, but as you start dreaming these dreams your energies will blend together and create a wonderful new reality on our planet. It is important that you do not leave this task exclusively to the beings of the Light Realms and to us in Telos. We have already created our world of paradise and we live in it. It is now your opportunity to create the world of your dreams. Your participation as co-creators is of the utmost importance. Creating a new reality for yourselves will allow you to achieve full mastery.

In your meditations and writings, we suggest that you to spend some time every day defining your perception of Heaven on Earth. Figure out what it means to you and start dreaming it. Dream of this new Earth at night as you fall asleep and dream about the new Earth during your waking hours as well. Imagination is the creative spark that fuels your manifestation. It connects you with the fluid reality of the realms of creation.

The more detail you include in your dreams, the more alive your dreams will become. Be as creative as you wish. The more real you make the vision, by investing your energies and uniting with your heart, the sooner Heaven on Earth will begin manifesting. Most of you are much too complacent.

Some of you hope that the Star Brothers and the Inner Earth populations will create all the magic for you.

If we did, what would you learn? Be assured that it will not happen this way. We come to assist you and the planet, yes, but it is up to you to do your part. Unless you choose to evolve your consciousness, raise your vibration and manifest greater levels of mastery, we will remain in the realm of the invisible.

Heaven on Earth is, in essence, a fifth dimensional reality. In the fourth dimension, life is much easier than in the third. The fourth dimension is much brighter and more fluid, but does not represent the full reality of Heaven on Earth. Begin with what you perceive to be a fifth dimensional reality, even if you are not quite sure what it consists of. Do your best and your consciousness will soon open to even greater perception and understanding.

Conscious dreaming brings about a progression of thoughts, an evolution that will take you, if you give permission, into this new dimension. The most important thing is to begin the process. Mother Earth has dreamed Her dreams. Now she is asking humanity to dream with Her to bring about the changes that you all yearn for.

Ask yourself these questions: What kind of life do I want? What type of government do I want? What kind of body do I wish to live in and how do I want to look? What type of system of exchange would I like to see evolve on the planet? Do I still want to use money as a means of exchange or would I prefer a more evolved type of barter system? Can I dream of something that no one has thought of before as a new and brilliant kind of exchange?

How would I like my relationships to be in the future? What will the Earth look like? What would the ideal climate be like? What will the animals look like and what will the new relationship between humans and animals be in the new world? There is no limit to what you can create. Have fun creating your own mental movies!

***Your imagination is a vast pool of memories
from everywhere you have ever been, from
many, many worlds through eons of time.***

Nothing that you can imagine is illusion. The images, for
most of you, are remembrances of past experiences stored
in an orderly, or sometimes not so orderly, manner. Sort
through this imagery and use all or part of it to create your
vision of a new reality. Access your deepest passions and
your buried remembrances of times and places long gone.
Touch your deepest self, and the images and ideas will flow.

The world offers itself to you,
And it is with Divine Love
That you receive this offering.
Your imagination is a conduit
To the part of your soul that
Recognizes and allows this love
To permeate your entire being.
        - Celestia

Chapter Two

The Last Wars on This Planet
A Candle of Hope

Greetings, my dear friends, this is Adama.

I am so grateful to be with you again. Tonight, I want to gift your hearts with a "candle of hope" and give you a broader perspective on the conflicts that are taking place on your planet. There are many from Telos joining me as I speak, for the purpose of enfolding you in a wondrous blanket of love, peace and protection.

Many people on the surface live in fear, anger and distress over these events that have the potential to create injustice and violence against humanity. You are wondering why these conflicts could not be stopped in view of the great love offerings, prayers, meditations and peace marches that millions of people have initiated on the planet. You wonder why the diligent efforts of so many brave souls, who have given all they have in an attempt to secure peace for the Earth and Her precious children, have not been enough.

It is not that, as a collective, you have not done enough. Believe me! You have done all you could, and your Creator has heard your prayers and cries for help and witnessed

9

your intention to live on a peaceful planet. Never in the history of the planet has humanity come together in such a grand way to demand Peace for the Earth. All of heaven has been watching in awe, praising your efforts and adding to them energetically. With the love and the solidarity you have demonstrated, you have attracted the attention of billions of space brothers from many universes and galaxies, who have come here to watch you and to energetically support your efforts to create peace on Earth.

In Telos, we have been keeping prayer vigils around the clock with all of you. We have made ourselves available to assist your safe passage into the next step of your evolutionary process in order to ease your pain, difficulties and worries.

Understand that there is a small group of people on the planet who arrogantly believe they "own this planet." They also believe they can do anything they please, no matter what the cost or how much pain and suffering is imposed on humanity and the Earth. In order to maintain the status quo of manipulation, domination and control, they need to keep all of you in servitude, in whatever manner and to whatever extreme you allow them to do so. They intend to maintain their enjoyment of 90% of the wealth of this planet while the rest of humanity struggles to survive on the remaining 10%.

> ***Those in control, dear ones, have a
> personal agenda. They want these
> conflicts more than anything else.***

The path to power is a strange one. Those who are driven by greed and the need to dominate misuse the Earth's resources. They ignore the call of the Divine within that guides them to serve the greater good. Their actions spring not from the heart of unity, but from fear and separation of their altered ego.

Those, on the other hand, who view the goal of power as an increase in perception and spiritual awareness join themselves with the flow of God. The more they embrace the unity of all life the more they evolve their consciousness and embody their true Divine Self. From the perspective of the true Master, war is not an option, not as a tool for learning nor as a viable opportunity for growth.

Eventually we will join with you in a more tangible way and the long dark night that has separated us for so long will be over. Together we will create our dream of a new wondrous world where only love and grace reside. Soon, those who hold the reins of manipulative power on this planet will be completely removed. Understand that they are aware that their time of control is coming to an end.

The Creator has already taken this precious planet back into His embrace and you are now under the jurisdiction of the Great Central Sun. These rulers know very well that the decree to end their dominance has been issued from the Great Central Sun. Nevertheless, out of desperation, they cling to the hope that they may succeed in a last attempt for total world control and domination.

> ***Recognize that they are ready to risk
> "everything" in an attempt to delay a
> little longer their day of accountability.***

Without any evidence of crimes, they are still accusing others in order to validate their own actions. Without the support of the rest of the world, they go ahead with their plans; but know in your hearts, my precious friends, the time of ruthless patriarchal dominance is coming to an end. They will soon be accountable for their actions against humanity. Be aware that their fears are far greater than yours. That is why they are so determined to play their "last card." And I do mean "their last card." They do not have any more after this.

11

It is now time for many of your political leaders to start experiencing a serious reduction of their power and tyranny. Divine Law does not allow interference with "free will." The spiritual hierarchy will allow events to follow the present course until such time as divine intervention is needed. Such intervention will come when the balance of humanity recognizes the choices made each and every moment which, in fact, support the old paradigm and choose instead to embrace a new way. When this shift occurs, "miracles" will take place everywhere. All is in readiness in the Light Realm to assist you in wondrous ways. It is only for you to decide and give permission.

Whatever the warlords ultimately do, the energies supporting their efforts are declining. Be at peace, for their war plans will not escalate to the level of a full world war. You have already laid the groundwork for a greater consciousness shift than even we had hoped for at this time. Each day more lightworkers join your ranks. Each day more awaken to their true nature and finally face the truth of their world. Your time has come, although world events may not seem to mirror this. Do not despair, for all is in alliance with you and your goal of harmony.

In the time of Lemuria we faced a similar situation when we experienced a long period of war between Atlantis and Lemuria.

Even in the face of the potential threat of total destruction of both continents, the warlords would not stop. The rest is history, and you all know what happened. You also know that there were no winners, as the wars weakened both continents to such an extent that both perished 15,000 years later. Many of the souls responsible for initiating the wars between Atlantis and Lemuria and their eventual destruction are the same souls presently attempting to do it once more.

This time, however, the situation is different. Your Earth

Mother's time for ascension has come and her wishes will be honored. From this time forward she will cleanse herself. She will no longer tolerate the abuse of Her body and of Her precious children. We ask you to allow Her the cleansing through the Earth changes. The third dimension will eventually roll its energy into the fourth dimension. There will no longer be a third dimension, as you know it today. Your body will mutate to a fourth dimensional body and later on to a fifth dimensional one which will be much lighter, but will still feel as physical. Closer than ever, you now stand at the dawn of a golden age of love and true brotherhood.

In the Light Realms we can now say that these impending conflicts are the last ones that will ever be waged on this planet. The dark forces know that they have reached their very last hour because the bells of accountability have been ringing in their ears for quite some time. They know that their only choice is to align with the consciousness of love or ship out. You've heard the expression "the beast roars the loudest when cornered." The Lightworkers in the United States and many other countries are banding together through the Internet and other means to create a web of light, unity and love. Those who hide in the darkness and veil their actions can see this web of light and love being created across and around the planet.

Your Light has become their greatest fear.

It is their desire not only to control the planet's oil supply, but also to destroy this web of light and love you are creating together. Their main agenda is to create circumstances that enslave the human race in a cage of fear. They want to keep you in a place of spiritual ignorance, emotional stress and financial poverty. In these ways they have succeeded quite well. Your life on the surface is quite challenging. Their plan is to use a few more terrorist attacks to engulf you in fear and control you for "your own good and safety."

13

Be at peace and hear the good news. Prior to your incarnation, your Creator promised that you would be allowed in this very lifetime to embody the fullness of your God Presence and your Christhood. You will be allowed to manifest on Earth, in your present incarnation, the fullness of your divinity and spiritual gifts which have been hidden from you for so long.

Understand that the beings controlling your planet propose to stop this developing enlightenment at all costs since it will bring their reign to an end. As the dark forces strive to bring all of you and the planet into greater servitude and increase your allegiance to separation and fear, the polarity of Light will at the same time create awakening and enlightenment. Even the planetary bodies in the heavens have aligned to facilitate this great surge in consciousness.

Soon those who are destined to form new governments and economic structures will become more visible. They have been preparing for this day and are already living among you. Do not judge them harshly or create expectations about them, for many who step forward may surprise you. Many have masked their true identities from within the very groups they seek to replace. Reach out with your hearts to recognize who your new leaders may be. All new structures will be formed for the benefit of the collective. This is an important key to identifying those who are finally ready to really support humanity. Even national borders will not stop those who support true change from coming together.

These conflicts will initiate an acceleration on the entire planet and assist in awakening millions to a new awareness of their divinity and a reconsideration of new values in their lives. Multitudes will discover new goals and purposes more aligned with their divine nature. As a result of these conflicts you will find millions of people swelling the ranks of the lightworkers and banding together to create permanent peace and a new reality based on divine truths.

These conflicts will also assist in eroding the outmoded patriarchal structures that no longer serve you. Be prepared to experience some sorrow and to witness the suffering that will take place. This will assist in opening your heart and easing your passage into the higher dimension. You will also clear much accumulated karma, making way for the new order and the recognition of your true Divine Self.

Children of my heart, allow the hand of God to wield its magic. Your Creator is watching attentively, protecting the Earth and Her people who have chosen to remain and embrace their new glorious destiny. Instead of going into fear, despair and hopelessness, light a candle of hope in your heart. Know that beyond war, a brand new world awaits. Miracles are just waiting to manifest. The gifts of love and grace from the Creator and your star family will pour down in ways you have never experienced before.

In your heart, light the candle of knowingness that the Divine will prevail and victory is assured.

People on this planet have stood together by the millions and stated their intention for peace, and so it shall be. You are marching across your planet demanding peace, and so it shall be. You have become the focus of the entire cosmos. We watch you, with love, intention and bravery rise up against the tyranny of one world government, saying, "This far and no further; your day is done." The Creator and all of you co-Creators are smiling, saying, "At last they are waking up; let there be peace on Earth, and so it shall be."

As the vibration continues to increase upon the planet, so will your responsibilities. We, your Lemurian brothers and sisters, are gathering our teams on the surface to implement our plans with many of you in every corner and country of this planet. Eventually, we will be working in good will with all who desire to serve the greater good with us. Nothing will be imposed on you. Your desire to serve with us must be ignited by the calling of your heart.

If you wish to be of service, our mission will involve great numbers of people. Many wondrous opportunities will offer themselves for those desiring to work with us side by side. You are the way-showers, the nucleus of many small groups that we are nurturing, embracing and cherishing here in Mount Shasta. The time of joy you have been waiting for is just beyond the clouds, beyond the storms of fabricated wars. If you can allow the clouds and storms to play out this last game, this last illusion, you shall never regret it.

Keep the candle of hope lit in your heart, for beyond the dark clouds is joy, ease and grace.

The dawning of a new world of unity and love, where violence no longer exists, is now just beyond the horizon. Take care of each other in times of need. Extend your love and comfort to those who have not had the opportunity to learn what you already know.

Become the pillars of peace for all those in fear, so that they can lean on you for comfort. As others lean on you, we invite you to lean on us for your strength and support. In the days to come, we will be close to you, extending much love and assistance.

Chapter Three

Connections between France, Quebec and Brazil

Adama, Celestia and the High Council of Telos

What is the connection between France, Quebec and Brazil?

Long before the existence of the underground city of Telos, there was a triangle of Mother energy which is now identified on the surface as the France, Quebec and Brazil triangle. Almost every area of the planet forms part of a triangle *(or trinity)* with two other parts of the planet. These grids are part of the Sacred Plan, which we use inside the Earth to assist in balancing and harmonizing the vibrations of the surface.

Each of these countries, although we do not refer to them as such inside the Earth, carries a particular vibration, a color, a sound harmonic and a planetary code. Together, all three create a new vibration and color that represents the grid's signature within Earth's interior, on the surface, and into the etheric planes that encircle the planet. It is important that this signature be recognized, because it serves in harnessing the energies of that particular grid. It also assists in harmonizing this grid with the energies of other grids on the planet. This network of grids interfaces with the organic meridian system of the planet herself.

17

As we traverse the network of grids from within the planet, we can take the pulse of the Earth in terms of the vibrations that are currently carried on the surface. These grids also assist us in the important work of monitoring energetic conditions throughout different regions of the Earth's Interior. It allows us to deflect many potentially catastrophic situations, man-made or elemental in nature, that would occur on the surface if an appropriate balancing of energies were not generated from within the Earth.

In terms of the energies of these three "countries" individually, on the surface you would recognize their vibrations as follows:

France

France transmits a glowing pink color which seems almost white on the edges, with the warmest pink in the heart of the country, the Paris region. The lightworkers who have incarnated in France during this time of planetary transformation carry within them the pure vibration of the Heart of Lemuria. While we recognize that all regions of the planet also host beings who carry these same vibrations, an extraordinary number of them have chosen to incarnate in France at this time. They have also incarnated in great numbers in the other two countries mentioned above, as children of the Lemurian Goddess, representing the consciousness of the heart and the love of Lemuria.

These choices were made in part because of the trauma that has engulfed France for most of the previous three centuries through several major wars and a revolution, which changed forever the government structures of France. In particular, the lasting effects of World War II created a need for more energetic balancing of the energies of the Jewish race in this region. The beliefs that much of the world has held regarding the Jewish race throughout this current period of civilization are incorrect.

The Jewish race has held the energies of the Divine Masculine in the consciousness of the Earth since mankind first appeared on this planet. This is not to say that others have not also carried Christed energies on this planet. The Jewish race was maintained as a true genetic race to uphold the pure spark of the Divine Masculine. In this regard the Jewish race is an integral part of the Lemurian identity, which has maintained within its culture this connection with Divine Source on this planet. We recognize that the vibration carried by the Jewish race has held its integrity through millennia of attempts to distort it. This was accomplished by requiring that the lineage be passed on through the mother in order to hold the structure and integrity within the DNA of the race.

As with all the many religions on the surface, the present-day dogma of the Jewish religion no longer holds the original vibration transmitted from the Divine eons ago. The source vibration itself has been held within the consciousness of the being that is your Earth Mother, and provides an ongoing identity for her. This source vibration is also held within the DNA of all beings who have had lifetimes of incarnation within the Jewish race, including the eras of Lemuria and Atlantis. This source vibration is present, to some extent, within most beings currently incarnated on this planet. The Hebrew language holds much source energy vibration and has been a part of many teachings and transmissions that have been rediscovered in your recent past. These ancient teachings are now fully investigated and available once again to the world.

Quebec

Quebec also carries a profound connection to this vibration. The colors that emanate from Quebec display a combination of peach, with a core of emerald green at the center. The heart of Quebec resides in the region of Montreal. Much is being done at this time to ready Montreal for the creation of a center from which to disseminate Lemurian teachings and healing work. The French-speaking population of Quebec has maintained their language as a heart connection to the heart vibration of France. Quebec was originally fashioned as an outpost for that vibration and a point of the triangle that transmits energies directly toward the North Pole of this planet. This connection to the pole is also one of the grid characteristics that allows transmissions of energies from the Earth's interior into the triangle, and from there into other parts of the overall grid.

Although the religion of this province became predominately Catholic, as did France, Quebec (Montreal in particular) holds an important connection to the Jewish race. Many who were persecuted in the last century in Germany for their Jewish heritage chose to reincarnate there in order to maintain their link to the heart vibration of Lemuria and escape the trauma of their previous incarnation. The healing energies of the province of Quebec are extraordinary. Many beings who have served throughout the eons as healers and teachers of these arts are now gathered to share this knowledge with the world.

The proximity of Quebec to the United States is also very important. Each of the three countries or regions forming a part of this trinity is connected directly to another country that holds, from the past, tremendous energies of destruction, violence and separation from Divine Source, at governmental and administrative levels. France holds this connection to Germany and Brazil holds it to Argentina. In each of these instances, the feminine heart energies of France, Quebec *(as well as other regions of Canada)* and Brazil are present to balance the overwhelming distrust of the feminine that the distorted patriarchal governments of the United States, Germany and Argentina hold.

Many of the perpetrators of great violence during the Second World War in Germany escaped retribution in their countries by traveling to the United States and Argentina.

They have helped to engender a vibration of distrust, violence and chaos. This distrust has formed a very important part of the vibration of anti-Semitism in these countries. This energy and the acts that have been allowed in its name are all attacks of the Divine Masculine in fear of the Divine Feminine.

In fact, these three countries (Germany, Argentina and the United States) form their own triangle of energies, allowing much imbalance and disharmony to spread throughout them. Their re-connection to the heart energies of Lemuria is facilitated through the grid of France, Quebec and Brazil re-establishing a greater level of harmony in these regions. This has been our greatest tool.

The energies against the Jewish race that have been dominant in the United States, Germany and Argentina attest to the high level of balancing that is going on at this time on the planet. Those who have the highest levels of distrust are moving into greater levels of fear as the light of the Divine grows brighter each passing day. In truth, many who have been incarnated in other lifetimes as Jews, even if they are currently not of that race, will be called into service as holders of that vibration. This blending of the true Divine spark of inspiration with the Goddess energy of the planet is unprecedented since Earth's creation.

Brazil
Brazil forms the link to the South Pole of the planet. The colors she emanates are very pleasing to the eye and include a combination of yellows, reds, blues and all the colors within the surface spectrum that these three primary colors can create. This is due to the highly crystalline nature of Brazil. She is in fact one very large, highly prismatic, generating crystal. Brazil is the transmission engine of the heart and healing energies emanating from France, Quebec and the Northern hemisphere of the planet into the Southern hemisphere.

The work that is currently being done within these three countries reflects the great number of highly evolved souls who have incarnated there at this time to hold the energies and serve the purposes of this very important grid. The heart energies of Lemuria manifest through this grid into the surface regions of the planet that need it most. The feelings held by many that these regions will be the first to be contacted directly by those from the Earth's interior and the Star Brothers is indeed true. In fact, this first level of emergence has already happened due to the great number of beings who have incarnated, or "walked into" these countries. It is now just a matter of these gatherings coming into greater light.

Those who so eagerly wish to contact you are in fact other aspects of "you" in another time, space and dimension. Many of you are physical extensions of souls who are present within the Earth or in other galaxies and universes. The more aspects of your multi-dimensional selves you can communicate with and integrate, the sooner the surface environment will recognize and reflect this.

We are already together in the vibrations of the crystalline grid and the network of grids that recognize the vibration of the heart inside and outside the planet. In truth, there is no distinction made between the dimensions when you travel the energies of this grid. We invite you all to connect with this network as readily and as often as you can, until it becomes a part of your intrinsic nature. The children who are incarnating today carry the key to this grid in their DNA and are working to share that key with all who live on the surface. Listen and open your hearts to them. They are envisioning a more highly evolved potential future for the planet than the majority of you would allow yourselves to imagine. We are all here in service of a Divine Plan and the love that we hold for you travels that path always.

Many blessings to you all. We wish you much joy for the next phase of your journey to love and freedom.

Chapter Four

The Magnetic Grid Work

Question: Adama, you revealed that you are involved in grid work. Please tell us what grid you are working on and what your role is in this work.

Blessings, beloved friends, I am Adama. You are truly masters who have joined together in this grand experiment. It is indeed the first time on this planet that consciousness has been raised through the integration of physical, emotional, mental and spiritual bodies concurrently.

I am involved in an energy grid inside the planet that works with the physical crystalline structure on the surface of the planet. This grid has to do with the planet herself. The energies from this grid go out from within and form an etheric grid around the planet, focusing on the vibrational raising of energy and with planetary shift. This action is also assisted by various activations from astrological configurations.

This grid is connected with Piscean energy and is used to hold the Christ energies. In the past it was used to hold the energies of the planetary grid. Now it has been upgraded to shift into Aquarian energy. As we begin to turn back towards the Great Central Sun through the raising of consciousness, these energies are shifting to a more Aquarian, feminine vibration. This does not mean that the masculine

23

is being lost. It simply means that both polarities are being integrated back into balance.

The vibration that comes out of Lemuria, especially out of Telos, is in itself a great generator of energy because of its position within Mount Shasta, an embodiment of the Great Central Sun on the planet. It is from within the mountain that all energies showered on your planet from the galactic core and the Milky Way hit the planetary grid. From here, in a matter of seconds, these energies hit all other major planetary points on the grid situated on mountaintops. From these points, the energies are distributed over the rest of the grid. Each grid has various entry and exit points. The exit points correspond to the areas where the energy is disseminated to other grids and planetary energy pathways.

The grid created by the Lemurian consciousness is also mirrored in each one of you. It is integrated into the sacred geometry of your body as you set your intention for the higher focus of divine purpose. There is now on the planet a division of energies between personal and global consciousness. Although both levels of consciousness are in truth one and the same, for the time being, there is an individuation between the two. This allows the vibrational shift in each individual to take place through free choice. This understanding was reached by the Lemurian High Council to reinforce on a cellular level the true dimensionality of this shift and fuse it into the collective consciousness of the human race.

Prior to this decision, it was thought that the global shift could happen with a series of infusions of energy to the planet herself, and then from the planet to you individually. However, you, as cells of the body of the planet, must anchor and integrate those vibrations individually to fully account for all of the unique permutations of human consciousness. The DNA matrix *(or crystalline grid)* will shift in a slightly different manner for each individual. In doing so, it will hold the full spectrum of vibrations needed for a true global shift. As energies then harmonize for larger and larger groups who have accomplished their individual shifts, the global shift will happen in ever-increasing waves.

There is a sound that accompanies this shift. This sound is generated in the etheric realms, but it can be heard on this plane. We call it the "song of the soul." Harps and lutes cannot produce as beautiful a sound as this wave of love that stirs within the soul and tickles the vibration of the heart and eardrums simultaneously. We have a three-stringed instrument in Telos that is played by caressing the strings, rather than plucking them, with our fore and middle fingers. This beautiful and inspirational vibration resonates in the same spectrum as soul songs.

As the grid accelerates, changes in your DNA matrix take place in each one of you. It will allow your own song to be heard. You all resonate to your own unique song that we often sing to you in recognition. It is like other titles and names you have that signify who you are by vibration. We truly celebrate you as you rediscover your songs. We grace your dreams with reminders in song to help you on your path. Our love joins together with yours for the grace of all.

What is your role in the grid work?

My work has to do with holding and feeding the grid with higher fourth and fifth dimensional energy vibration that is gradually brought up to the surface from within. We work within the planet to help the energies rise through the planet herself. When you connect with the Earth, physically or subtly, you can feel the energy that way. We also release energetic enhancements out through the north and south poles and other key points.

My role is one of administrator, architect of the grid and organizer of energy input and releases. As the structure of the grid itself is now in place, my work involves further modifications to enhance the flow of energies. The grid is constantly evolving, a continuous work in progress!

There are many, many beings also working with the grids. There have been references made to different grids, but they are in fact multi-dimensional layers of one huge, extensive grid work that is being integrated now.

What is the difference between the Kryon grid and your grid?

Different energies work with different components of setting-up the grid. Kryon works primarily with the magnetic energy of the grid and we work with the crystalline energy. However, this work is a coming together of different groups who have worked with these energies over a long period of time, each contributing different components to the grid. The new grid has been created as a result of the participation of many, many different energies, including the Elohim, Arcturians, Pleiadians, Andromedans, Venusians and even star energies and races that cannot be identified easily in your frame of reference. As we are all parts of a whole, this grid is being formed as one whole to serve the planet and humanity.

Within the grids being unified at this time, there are many different entry and exit points. You as individuals bring a unique piece to each joining together of energies in which you engage, thereby creating a new and unprecedented effect. So to, this grid is creating a new field around the planet that will hold and harvest the wonderful energies being generated to and through the Earth. These energies are not just one-time transmissions, but will continue to form and hold around the planet in an ongoing process.

Is the plan to restore the planet to its original state of perfection or to move beyond that?

It is certainly the plan and hope that more magic will be created here than any of us can imagine. There is still a question about how the planet is actually going to evolve. All is dependent on the extent of shift possible in the human consciousness, individually as well as collectively. How much of this wondrous plan will you allow to unfold? How much will you choose to co-create with us? As we experience the great shift of feminine energy on the planet, how much resistance will be encountered? Will you continue to tear down that which we are actively trying to re-build? At this point, much is still seriously in question.

It is also a matter of what you choose to do to assist this process and how you choose to live as citizens of this planet. The magnetic grid has shifted and the crystal grid has been reborn. Now we are all waiting for the quickening of the next great grid, the grid of human consciousness, before we can proceed further with the work. There is so much that is going to happen in the next ten years in terms of consciousness-raising. It is important to see communities come together and demonstrate their full support of the Earth.

What shift in human consciousness is needed for you to emerge to the surface?

We have a plan for our emergence that we cannot disclose at this time. Our plan remains flexible with various potentials, and which one will actually unfold will depend on how humanity shifts. We would like to see humanity begin to live from the heart at all times, rather than this "wait and see" attitude.

Some people who hear about us rationalize in their minds, rather than finding the truth deep in their hearts, and decide they will believe only when they see us in front of them. Our eventual emergence is contingent on everyone raising his or her own level of love and light vibration and in living from the heart.

When people's heart connection with us becomes more constant, then we will be present in a more consistent way. Those with the "wait and see" attitude will certainly have to wait much longer to see us. For quite some time yet, your physical presence among us will be permitted "by invitation only." As previously explained, these meetings will not take place in a third dimensional vibration. It is up to you to raise your vibration.

As the energies continue to shift on the planet, this shift in vibration will soon be possible for many of you drawn to this material. We have by now witnessed great heart openings, acceptance and heart-felt welcome from the French populations of this planet through the publishing of our books. This is giving us great hope that soon we will be able to initiate small clandestine gatherings with those who have reached the level of vibration necessary to be in our presence.

We ask you to let go of your old 3D distorted energies and move up to a new level of love and joy. This is the key.

Chapter Five

The Effects of Recreational Drugs on Spiritual Development

A Dialog with Adama

Example: Marijuana and other narcotics. The same principles apply in great measure to all other addictions such as alcohol and tobacco.

Aurelia - Adama, is there a group consciousness attached to the use of and addiction to substances such as marijuana or peyote as recreational drugs and/or spiritual tools? Please describe what effect these substances have on their users.

Adama - I would like to speak first on the general use of recreational drugs. A little history to begin with, if you will! When these sacred plants originally came forth from Creation they had the wonderful purpose of uplifting energy and consciousness.

In the beginning of their use a long time ago, consciousness-altering plants assisted people to open their perception to their divine qualities, to their divine Presence and Creator. These plants were used also to enhance telepathic abilities, as well as the gifts of clairaudience, clairvoyance, psychometry and other similar spiritual abilities.

These spiritual openings connected people more directly

29

with the angelic kingdom, nature spirits, the animal kingdom and beings from the other side of the veil. The enhanced energies provided by the use of the sacred plants also facilitated inter-dimensional travel. These were the main purposes of these herbal substances, to create spiritual pathways. This is the way it was in the beginning of creation before the "fall in consciousness" that took place during the fourth golden age.

The original sacred plants assisted the spiritual evolution of mankind in the beginning of life on this planet for millions of years, until the fourth golden age. During this long period of Earth evolution, people would occasionally draw on the energies of these plants with much reverence, sacredness and intention. They ate a small portion of a leaf, usually directly from live plants, according to the experience that was desired. There were a variety of these plants, each one offering its own specific spiritual gift. At no time were the plants misused, nor was addiction experienced from their use.

Children were given a full understanding of their use at a young age, and their intended use was always honored. The sacred plants vibrated at a fifth dimensional frequency and beyond. People did not smoke to inhale these substances through their lungs, as is done today. The present-day counterparts of these original plants, by the way, are not the same plants at all. Depending on the species, a specific portion of the leaf was required and consumed to attain the desired results. People approached the plants with much reverence, asking permission of the plant Devas to partake of the attributes each plant carried.

These plants grew abundantly in many places, and almost every home had a sacred spot in the garden reserved for the growth of a small quantity of a few species. They were considered food for the soul, just as important as food for the body. The sacred plants carried a very high vibration. When ingested, they shared attributes of their vibration that elevated the body and opened the consciousness to higher understandings and experiences. The so-called "weed" that this generation smokes or uses today with the hope of connecting with a higher aspect of themselves or experiencing other-dimensional realities, are not, in any way, the same as those originally used for spiritual purposes. The original plants no longer exist in your third dimensional reality, although several species have been preserved inside the Earth.

Incarnated beings practicing the black arts were the first to genetically alter the original plants.

To understand what happened with this gift that mankind used freely for so long it is necessary to go back in history to the beginning of the dark ages, when people consistently gave away their power to lesser vibrations other than their own Divine Presence. One by one, the civilizations of this planet gradually forgot their original state of oneness with the divine and opened themselves to the manipulating and controlling energies of the shadow.

Incarnated beings of the black arts, who had acquired great knowledge on other spheres of existence prior to coming to the Earth, became the black magicians of ancient times. They are the ones who first genetically altered the sacred plants at their roots. By doing so, they exercised greater and greater control over people by dimming their spiritual powers and perceptions. This took place over a long period of time; the vibrational rate of the original plants was gradually destroyed or greatly reduced. The plants available today for "recreational use" carry a negatively altered vibration that is a far cry from the original ones.

The youth and many adults on this planet are addicted to substances that take their users into the lower levels of the astral plane. In the lower astral realms, users get hooked and corded by astral entities needing their energies in order to survive. These are the major cause of addiction. Those indulging in these substances endlessly create these distorted energies in the emotional and other subtle bodies. These entities exist with a consciousness of their own. They are real and alive, living in a low energy consciousness that becomes more and more aggressive in its attempt to gain control of the user. Over time and with continued use, the entities grow in number and in power in the energetic field of their hosts.

These low vibrational entities have so little light and energy of their own that they "have to get hooked" on "willing" human beings and produce cravings in the emotional body to survive. The cravings are the fundamental roots of addiction, created by entities of the astral plane that suck your light and your energies whenever they can to assure their own survival. One can say that your addictions are also "their fix." How so many types and levels of addiction are formed is not well understood. If it were, few of you would partake of addictive substances, not even plain commercial cigarettes or alcohol.

What you have left today is a handful of low vibration, consciousness-altering plants. Instead of lifting people in consciousness to the realms of Light in their multi-dimensional travels, the negative qualities of the plants you have today take their users into the lower vibrations of the astral plane, where light is dim and consciousness distorted. The black magicians brilliantly altered the vibrations of the original plants to create a tearing effect in the soul and a greater separation from Source.

Recreational drugs users are, for the most part, people who perceive consciously or unconsciously that they have lost connection with their Higher Self. They are seeking a form of union at the emotional level with a greater part of themselves. Addictions arise from this natural desire of the soul, which can never be fulfilled by engaging in these kinds of activities. Drug users keep inhaling or ingesting more and more of the consciousness-altering substances in a desperate attempt to reconnect with a part of themselves that would fill the void and the emptiness they feel deep within themselves.

Drug use illustrates an attempt to find externally the Connection and the Love that can only be found within the Self, through the Love of Self that beats through your heart.

I repeat again, mind and soul altering substances found on the surface can only amplify the void, emptiness and loneliness of the soul who seeks fulfillment outside of the Self.

When one relies on a low vibration substance to create an altered state or to reconnect with the divine, the result is only greater illusion and self-deception. Do you understand that?

The grasses that are grown and the chemical substances that are produced today for mind-altering purposes are totally unnatural to the soul, the physical body, the mind and the emotional body. These substances create distortions in these bodies that can take a very long time to correct, even several lifetimes.

The original genetic state of sacred plants was love, innocence and purity. Now there is a huge group consciousness of drug entities that are destructive to the very fabric of life and consciousness itself. There is almost no place you can go now free from the vibration of these entities. This is another plot of the dark brothers, whose agenda is to stop or slow down the evolution of this entire generation. You find large groups of entities waiting for their "willing prey," clustered in areas where people gather to inhale or partake of these substances.

If you could observe from our perspective, you would know, without a doubt, that anyone indulging in these substances invites legions of these entities in. They cling to and torture their host emotionally to incite more consumption. They are like hungry vampires competing for their "fix." The addiction comes not so much from the plant itself but from the entities who attach themselves to those using these substances. This is the main cause of the torment of addiction.

*Aurelia - **What do these entities look like?***

*Adama - * I'm going to describe these entities to you. They look like thick smoke and can be six, ten, twelve or twenty feet long, and shaped a bit like a snake. They grow larger as the energy wraps itself around all the various bodies—physical, emotional, mental and spiritual—of those who partake of these substances. It is mainly the emotional body that is affected, as it gets imprinted with the constant craving for more and more drugs by the astral entities who embody that vibration.

Most of the time addiction leads to personality changes and character damage. The soul becomes more and more disconnected from the purpose of its incarnation and from the "real self." Those who spend their lifetime in this altered state may have to experience several more incarnations to return to the state they embodied before the drug use. They will almost certainly suffer a setback in their personal evolution. Some rationalize that their drug-induced "high" is actually the doorway to spiritual development, but we say that they are embracing a great illusion.

Aurelia - Can you be more specific about how each of our four bodies—emotional, physical, mental and spiritual—as well as the auric field, are affected by drug use?

On the emotional body

*Adama - * Of your four bodies, the one most affected is the emotional body. The entities lure people into addiction by creating a sensation of starvation or craving for the addictive substance primarily in the emotional body and the solar plexus. It is well documented that those who take these substances retard the growth and maturing of their emotional bodies. In general, they can remain quite unbalanced or immature emotionally for many years, or even the remainder of their incarnation. When you see men or women in their thirties and forties with the maturity of a 15 or 20-year-old, you know there is something that has stunted the growth of their emotional body. The emotional body usually stops maturing at the age one starts ingesting these substances. Often, you hear people say that someone is 43 years old going on 16 in maturity. Do you get the picture?

This emotional immaturity creates deficiencies in the character building of the drug user. Instead of developing the qualities of their divinity, the addiction causes many to resort to all sorts of manipulations, treachery and distorted ways of acquiring money in order to get another fix. There are those who will even kill or resort to prostitution to get the funds to feed their addiction. Drug dependency often destroys or diminishes the qualities of the soul, and the goals of the incarnation are not met.

Everyone has a certain desire to evolve and become the divine being they are. This is your very nature, your birthright. Those who use drugs or similar addictive substances are looking outside themselves for what can be found only within the depth of the soul. Drug abuse demonstrates an unwillingness to go through the normal channels of learning and the daily lessons of life that help you evolve. In all truthfulness, there are no external shortcuts to enlightenment. It is all within you.

As the vibration on the planet increases, the youth of the world and the users of recreational drugs will have to make a serious choice and commitment to their life, to their evolution and to the predetermined purposes of their incarnation. They will soon be faced with the choice to either awaken spiritually and "get of pot" or possibly leave their present incarnation and spend time in the astral plane with the destructive energies they have flirted with. Basically, at some point, this is the choice all will have to make if they wish to ride the wave of ascension and reunite with their Divine Selves.

On the mental body

In the mental body, drug use affects the character and level of integrity. The motives for living become very distorted. Instead of living for the development and integration of noble purposes, life often becomes an obsessive ratrace for money to buy more of these substances. The user's mind becomes dulled and cloudy while existing in this kind of consciousness. Genetically, drug use can often create repercussions in the progeny for two to three generations, which can manifest as various kinds of physical, emotional or mental weaknesses. Children born into families who inherit such problems may be souls who are choosing to resolve unfinished karma from their own addictions in a past incarnation.

On the physical body

On the physical level, drugs and any addiction lower all the vibrations of the body. There are those who are genetically very strong and don't seem to be physically affected. For many, the brain and the emotional body are most affected. Nevertheless, one must be aware that the person who indulges in recreational drugs for a long time and fails to fulfill their present life contract will most likely lose the privilege of a strong healthy body in the next incarnation. And you all know how painful and agonizing this can be!

You can never consciously or carelessly abuse your body in one incarnation and have the privilege of a healthy and strong body again in the next one. Divine law requires that if you are given a strong healthy body and you misuse it, the karma returns the very next life. That is why you have children born with all sorts of health problems. You wonder why is this? What did they do to deserve it? Well, on the human level you can never judge because you don't know the whole story. Even if you were to look at astrological or akashic records, the human consciousness can only perceive a small portion of the whole picture.

In general, people trapped in addictive tendencies tend not to feed their bodies what is needed to remain in balance and vitality. These types of imbalances created in the body are not conducive to motivating addicts to change their ways. They are malnourished, to say the least. Not feeding the body properly and regularly is part of the self-hatred and denial syndromes of those engaging in addictions. This means that they do not value themselves as divine beings, and do not value the opportunity for this life either. The body needs to be replenished several times a day with natural and nutritious foods that carry as much life force as possible. Junk food diets in the form of fast foods completely devoid of nutrients have been the main diet of the great majority of drug users.

On the etheric body

Etherically, drugs tear down much of the protective sheaths of the soul, known as subtle bodies. It could take a person who has indulged in one lifetime in the constant use of marijuana, LSD or other recreational drugs three to five lifetimes or longer to return to balance. Addictions can cause tremendous damage to the etheric bodies. From a physical perspective it is never obvious how much the non-visible bodies have been harmed. We are not talking about someone who has simply tried drugs as an experiment a few times and never continued; that will not hurt you deeply. We are talking about regular use over a long period of time.

Many of you have been using drugs for five to ten years or longer. At this time, because of the Divine Grace being offered to all of humanity by your heavenly Father, there is still time for all to let go of the addictions and begin a spiritual, emotional and physical cleansing. By divine grace, all can receive great healing. However, if the soul leaves this incarnation before healing takes place, many may take that damage into the next incarnation without full awareness of why problems manifest in their physical bodies.

Aurelia - How is the auric field affected?

Adama - From our perspective, when we look at a person who is a child of love, light and innocence, the auric field demonstrates a beautiful emanation of all the colors of love, the seven rainbow rays and golden light. It radiates out in different intensities of tone, and the auric field shows beautiful geometric patterns of colors of high vibration. It is so because the beautiful colors of God have their counterparts in the full spectrum of the rainbow.

When you look at the auric field of a user of marijuana or other drugs, you see very distorted patterns of the red tone of anger and vile green tones not representing harmony and love. There are also a lot of black and brown splashy spots all around the aura. More often than not, the beautiful original geometric auric pattern can no longer be seen. It is muddy in tone as the colors are very distorted. You would also see clusters of entities like coiling serpents of smoke wrapping themselves around every part of the body. The solar plexus and the heart become congested with these entities and their low frequency energy. The etheric body and auric field of users of recreational drugs are not a pretty sight. If we could show drug users their auric field compared to the one we described above, they would be shocked and might quit drug use on the spot.

Aurelia - Our DNA is now mutating back to its original 12-strand light-body as the Earth prepares to go into her ascension frequency. How does this new stage of human evolution affect people who are using these drugs?

Adama - Unfortunately, they are not mutating in a positive way. The main factor in cellular mutation is the love vibration and the effort the person puts into raising their vibration. How do you expect to raise your vibration while you are creating, feeding, maintaining and entertaining legions of negative entities?

Drug users constantly lower their vibration in order to feed these entities which, when one thinks about it, is really an act of self-hatred. The low vibration that users maintain is not conducive to increasing their love and light frequencies, thus inhibiting the mutation of their DNA into a higher state of evolution.

Your sustained love and light quotient is the determining factor in your DNA's automatic activation. This natural process has little to do with paying someone to do DNA activations, which often are ceremonies of intention. Unless the love and light frequency is increased and maintained by the receiver, not much can be accomplished.

The activation of your light-body is determined and accelerated by the amount of love and light you are able to maintain on a day-to-day basis. This includes the love of Self, the love of your body and the love for your incarnation's purpose.

Aurelia - Does the illegal status of marijuana in certain places affect its vibration? For example, is there a fear consciousness associated with its illegality?

Adama - Yes, definitely. Marijuana, the plant itself, possesses some positive applications if and when properly utilized. It is a question of letting go of fear and addiction and putting each thing in its right perspective. Marijuana is a variety of the hemp plant. Your authorities have made it illegal out of fear. The hemp plant could be used in many positive ways for the benefit of mankind. Instead, it is used in negative ways in an attempt to repress and regress the soul evolution of an entire generation.

The fact that it is illegal creates a greater interest or special attraction for the youth and many adults. Its illegal status creates fear and feeds the fear consciousness/entities within the self. For many who live with fear issues in their unconscious, doing something fearful stimulates the energy of the fear entities within the self, creating the false illusion of mental and emotional thrill.

Understand that drug entities are fed by the vibration of the altered plants, and fear entities are fed by fear energy. Being in fear and creating the fear vibration has become a form of addiction for a great many people. Why do you think so many people enjoy horror films or violent movies? Why are these types of attractions so popular? The emotions created by watching these scenes feed the fear entities that run the internal programming of those watching and enjoying the stimulating sensations. Those who have not made peace with their heart and their Divine Presence have not yet understood the true meaning of Love and Peace.

On this planet, the great majority of people are programmed to be emotionally activated by fear. This is part of an old, old program that now needs to be released by everyone committed to enlightenment. In the new consciousness and evolution humanity and the planet are travelling toward, there will be no room for such vibrations. Those still choosing to carry these vibrations will be held back and denied entrance until their lessons are learned. The fifth dimensional consciousness will not accept this kind of baggage from anyone.

Making drugs illegal doesn't resolve the problem. Those determined to use drugs will find a way of doing so. The clandestine way recreational drugs are marketed and the fact that they are illegal encourages users to become deceitful and dishonest with themselves and others. This is not said to criticize or judge the authorities. They tackle the drug problem to the best of their ability. Drug users become secretive and suspicious and live a double life. This behavior is certainly not conducive to building the human personality and character needed for ascension and evolution into higher consciousness.

The child of Light, the child of love and innocence, cannot find anything to hide.

Life on this planet is moving toward the consciousness of total knowingness and openness, where everything will be known and nothing will be hidden. Do you know that in the higher realms no one can hide anything because everything can be seen and known at all times through your auric field, your tone, your vibration and the colors you radiate? We can see everything in the auric field of all the people on Earth we choose to gaze upon, as well as in our own community of Light. Very soon, there will be no more secrets anywhere on this planet.

Come on, my friends, children of my heart, do you really think you can hide in your secrecy? Well, the truth is that you can not. Perhaps you can hide some things for a while from other fellow humans; but you simply cannot hide any secrets, thoughts, feelings or intentions from any one of us of the Light Realm, anywhere above the third dimensional consciousness.

Even the trees, the nature spirits and the animals can easily read your heart, your intentions, your past and your future. If you were telepathic or if they could speak to you in a language you understood, you would be quite surprised at their wisdom and knowledge. This will soon change for most of you as you evolve. As humanity opens its heart to unconditional love and acceptance of others, this type of communication with all of life, which all beings of enlightened civilizations enjoy presently, will open up for you as well and you will enjoy this new magic tremendously. Never will you be afraid of anything anymore. You will know that peace has always been there beneath your fears.

My words may appear harsh or exaggerated for some of you. But believe me, all I have described has become a reality for too many precious souls. Not all those using marijuana will experience every symptom I have described. I have tried to show you the path that drug use leads to when alignment with the incarnation's true purpose continues to be ignored.

Aurelia - Is there anything people can do to heal themselves from the abuse of marijuana or similar types of substances? What healing tools can you recommend?

Adama - Well, sweet one, we wish we had a magic potion or miracle solution. Vibrational healing tools are emerging that will be of significant use to healers and counselors in the coming years. These devices, some of which are already in limited use, accelerate the clearing and rebuilding of the etheric body. In the hands of a practitioner who is aligned with the Divine, they will greatly assist all who desire to process and purify old distorted energies. They will also provide great assistance to the children incarnating now who are experiencing tremendous stress in your surface societies. These children are not only relying on mind-altering substances that are illegal, but are being fed such substances by doctors under the guise of treatment for ADD syndromes and other mental diseases.

It is unfortunate to witness in so many countries the dark forces have swayed children born as indigo and/or violet souls into addiction to these habit-forming substances. This sinister plan is designed to bind their souls and stop the wondrous contribution and wisdom they are meant to bring to this planet. This is a trap too much of the youth of this world is falling into. Nearly all of those precious souls come here at this time of Earth transition with mighty goals and great missions. We know that a great percentage of these precious children will awaken in time. However, for those who do not, the drug abuse and addiction will mark a major set-back in their evolution.

The right information and knowledge of the truth can begin to make a great difference. Unfortunately, peer pressure has played a very negative role in your society. It is the giving up of one's power and values to avoid appearing "different" or to feel "accepted" by others. I say to you, "Dare to be different! It is a sign of maturity and sovereignty."

Know that there is no one as effective as an ex-drug user in convincing others to stay clean.

Without a doubt, the time has come for incarnated souls to face the choice of "getting off pot" or leaving their present incarnation for a less evolved sphere of evolution where they can continue to learn their lessons. We hope that many, when faced with a final choice, will make the right choice. We realize, however, that you live in a society evolving on a planet of "free choice," where people are meant to experience and experiment freely. Remember that all the choices you make from day to day and the intentions you hold in your heart and mind have significant consequences for you now and for your future.

We ask you to pray for these precious children, for grace and divine intervention. We ask those who will be reading this material to enfold the youth of the world in a whirlwind of love, of blue and violet flame for their protection. We ask that you petition the Archangels for their protection. These spiritual tools are very, very important. If you know someone using drugs, or teachers open to concepts of higher consciousness, give them this information or communicate what you feel they will understand. Share your wisdom with them. Information and knowledge are some of the best tools to transform consciousness. You may not interfere with anyone's free will, but you may offer someone the gift of knowledge. It will allow that person to make an "enlightened" choice, perhaps for the first time.

Many people falsely believe they are on a high spiritual path by taking drugs.

Those who think they are on a high spiritual path by taking drugs because they experience an altered state do not realize that these experiences take them to lower levels of the astral plane. What they experience is a far cry from the joy and ecstasy of the etheric planes, the dwelling place of higher consciousness. There is a distinct difference between the astral plane and the realms of light. The etheric plane begins to be experienced, to some extent, at the higher levels of the fourth dimension, and then much more fully in the fifth dimension and beyond.

The astral plane is rightly called the plane of duality, relativity and spiritual unconsciousness where there is little or no light. All that one perceives is distorted and fragmented compared to the realms of light. In the astral plane, truth and divinity are no longer understood. It is also considered a giant pool for all the unfulfilled desires and negative emotions of mankind that have been created in separation from God. Consider it a place of great illusion. More often than not, it creates the illusion of a world containing beauty and pleasure that seduce souls away from their intended soul path. It projects all the deceptions of the human consciousness, at times very well camouflaged, and creates the appearance of something better than it actually is. The astral plane is always devious, distorted, alluring and deceitful.

The astral plane is comprised of different levels, from the highest level to the lowest, which some of you refer to as "the bottom of the pit." Until the astral plane is clear of human negativity, the vibrations will prevent anyone from reaching the etheric planes. Thus, drug use can never bring an experience of light unless the right substances carrying the right vibrations are used "appropriately." In your present world, children of my heart, the former sacred plants are either very rare or extinct.

The younger children of this generation are very brilliant and psychic. They know when they are told the truth and when they are deceived. They are born with higher levels of perception than most presently incarnated. Many of them who read our information will be able to recognize the truth of it and embrace it fully. Unfortunately, only some enlightened writings about the spiritual consequences of drug abuse have been published, but most of this information has eluded you or been suppressed.

The children of the world, young and old, need this information. Please spread the word; it is of the utmost importance. Many parents are not well prepared for their parenting roles and thus are too complacent with their children. Often they are too busy with the daily demands of their lives. Children in general do not receive the spiritual wisdom they need from their parents to grow and mature as divine beings in this physical realm. Parents are responsible for teaching their children true spiritual values.

Accurate teachings of true wisdom have been destroyed on this planet. This is why so much new information is pouring in from other dimensions and star systems, as well as from the Earth and her kingdoms in order to assist humanity in finding its way back to Source and Oneness. Those who destroyed the library of Alexandria in the early time of Christianity played an important role in keeping humanity in ignorance. This library contained well over 400,000 books holding much of the wisdom accumulated over eons of time and kept in sacredness to enlighten humanity. After this beautiful library was burned to the ground, humanity began to experience a "dark age" that lasted for many centuries.

Those who orchestrated the destruction of such a precious collection of spiritual wisdom and knowledge for the planet were very proud and happy with themselves at first. In their thirst for power and control they convinced themselves that they had performed an act of mercy for humanity. They sought to dim the light on the planet by depriving mankind of the very teachings that would show the way to a life of love, grace and the salvation of their souls. The destruction of those precious records created an enormous loss and set the evolution of the planet back. Those responsible for the obliteration of such treasures were instruments of the sinister forces. To this day they are reaping the karma of their actions.

Aurelia - Please comment on the effects of drug use on the chakras. Are they "blown" open when drugs are used?

Adama - That is not exactly what happens. Actually the chakras close to the light as they are being ripped apart. Prolonged drug use gradually creates weakening and tearing or misalignment of the chakra system. The chakras can no longer carry as much light and begin to be imprinted with negativity. That is why I mentioned that as many as five to ten lifetimes can be required to heal the imbalances. When the chakra system becomes imprinted with great negativity from the astral plane and the light dims, the healing forces are no longer present in the chakras.

The soul involved is often born with severe physical or emotional imbalances in the next few incarnations. With right action, self-love and willingness to improve oneself with each succeeding incarnation, the light begins to rebuild in the chakras and healing will eventually take place. The soul will find its way back to where it started in its evolution. It is like taking many steps backwards and then returning to your original starting place, a rather unnecessary and avoidable delay.

A soul is not accorded the same level of grace in the next incarnation when they choose to forsake their purpose and destiny to indulge in any type of addiction, especially a soul born with as much light as the children of today. For several lifetimes, these souls will experience life without the support of the beautiful light they now carry until they learn their lessons. That is why it has been said that souls engaging in drug use are embarking on a painful journey for many lifetimes to come.

Aurelia - Adama, this is a time of great grace for everyone on Earth. What opportunities are there for people who turn away from this type of distortion and desire to move into the light more rapidly?

Adama - Addiction and drug use were created on your planet as a plot of the dark forces. They are determined more than ever before to stop the expansion of the light and to prevent as many souls as possible from making it easily to the ascension door in this life. The precious children could make it so easily and painlessly! They were born with all the tools they need to attain their enlightenment and spiritual freedom with much ease and grace.

> **So many of the children addicted to drugs now need unprecedented assistance from enlightened adults who have the wisdom to understand that a whole generation of enlightened beings is at stake here.**

The new energy that now floods the Earth will not support that dark consciousness. The children will be granted an opportunity and a period of grace to align and heal completely so that they can come into the new world together with the rest of humanity. However, the children need to understand that they are responsible for making the ultimate choice for themselves; no one can make it for them. Those who choose to leave will become aware, when they cross to the other side of the veil, that they have forsaken a wondrous opportunity.

Knowledge, my sweet ones, knowledge and understanding are the greatest tools at this time. Offering these gifts to those who have not had the opportunity to receive this wisdom from those involved in their upbringing is indeed a great act of love and compassion.

Aurelia - Do you have some of the original sacred plants in Telos, and do you use them?

Adama - In Telos, many of the original plants have been preserved, and yes, we have plants that can assist spiritual development. We don't smoke them of course. We also do not need them. Our present level of spiritual consciousness far exceeds any benefit that these plants could offer us. We cultivate them for their beauty and grace, as we do so many other species. Don't forget, these plants have graduated to become fifth dimensional species!

At some point in the future we might consider assisting some of you with your openings through the "right use" of one or two of the plants we have preserved. Be assured that it will not be used with many. They will not be for sale in your markets either, nor available to those who now indulge in the use of the altered counterparts you grow.

It is certainly sad that a whole generation is being swallowed up by this drug consciousness. Be aware that it is the ultimate plan of the dark forces to wipe out this generation "spiritually" and enslave them if possible. Will you allow this to happen or will you wake up to the truth of who you are and why you are here?

Aurelia - Marijuana is also used for medical purposes. Does it matter how it is used? Does it always create damage?

Adama - Medical use and recreational use of marijuana are not the same thing. People in hospitals in severe pain take sedatives such as morphine or Demerol, which are other types of substances that stop or reduce pain. These substances are habit-forming, mind-altering and lower the body's vibration to that of the astral plane. Marijuana used for a short time as a medical prescription for pain, let's say after surgery, is not going to do the damage I have described. However, many years of unnecessary drug use cho-

sen as a way of life to avoid the lessons, responsibilities and challenges chosen for the incarnation can create spiritual consequences. There are those who have been on drugs for many years and have been able to stop and now are healing themselves. Much grace is granted to them.

Now, as it evolves, every incarnated soul has to eventually learn how to heal itself. This is part of the "mastery curriculum" you came here to complete. Many souls have made the choice to leave their embodiment in the next few years without having any clue about healing themselves. They will most likely go to another planet to continue their evolution and stay there until they learn to heal all of their imbalances. There are several other planets now willing to host these souls, where they will be taught in a different way what they did not learn here. They have eternity to evolve as they wish. Their free choice is always honored.

Aurelia - *Can you comment on how they can heal themselves?*

Adama - There are some who have given up their addiction "cold turkey" with a firm will and determination to heal themselves. They are receiving much grace and assistance from Above. It is important for them to invoke the healing light of their soul and reconnect with their Eternal Self as the great "I AM" on a daily basis. Going back to a healthy and natural diet will help keep them in balance and greatly ease the process. Active meditation and the use of the seven sacred healing flames will bring great mercy and grace to their life stream.

At this time, grace on this planet is distributed in an extraordinary way to anyone who is sincerely and wholeheartedly committed to healing themselves at all levels of their being. Once a person who has been a drug user for many years makes a firm commitment to life and remains clean, the angels of divine grace are at their side assisting.

On Earth at this time, you are literally running out of time. The question you need to ask yourself is: "Do I really want to extend my third dimensional challenges and lessons for another ten or more lifetimes somewhere else, living in pain and separation from my true Self? Do I want to wait for the next round of ascension, in perhaps 10,000 years on another planet? Or do I want to ascend now with the Earth and the rest of humanity to experience the glory of spiritual freedom and joy that will change my life experience forever?"

Aurelia - What about those who are not inhaling?

Adama - Those who do not inhale this energy through their lungs, but choose to keep company with those engaging in the drug use can experience, through this association, lowering of their own vibration.

Aurelia, you have been facing your shadow side; you have invested much effort in your own healing and you know how difficult and strenuous it has been. You have worked hard to heal your issues and imbalances and you know the difficulties you have encountered. Your emotional baggage was less than most. You are increasing your vibration in a wondrous way. You are opening your heart and your strands of DNA are evolving because your intention is pure and focused.

What does this tell you about what kind of self-healing work will be required of those who choose to remain in complete denial of what is required of them to fulfill the purpose for their present incarnation?

Aurelia - Can you comment on the importance of being in divine alignment for the current ascension cycle we are entering and the effects of the use of marijuana on alignment with the I AM?

Adama - Those believing that they will open up faster or

make greater spiritual progress with the assistance of drug use entertain total illusion. There are those who have had partial third eye openings with the use of drugs, but this is not true clairvoyance acquired through the discipline of the soul on the path of ascension and enlightenment. There are no shortcuts, dear sister. Everyone, without exception, has to accomplish their spiritual homework in the vibrations of love and light and clear all emotional issues and karmic baggage.

Those who have opened their psychic perceptions through drug use may have to accept a closing down of these faculties. Such openings not in alignment with true clairvoyance, but of lower vibrations, cannot be sustained. All legitimate openings must come about through the grace of your Divine Self when you are ready or when it is part of your preordained pathway. Let me share that almost 50% of people who have developed clairvoyant abilities do not own these gifts by divine appointment. For many, these skills create greater separation and illusion. I ask all of you reading this material to be careful and to use your discernment. Do not be deceived by that trap. When external means to reach spiritual alignment are relied upon, rest assured that a shadow of the "real truth" is created, not true spiritual brilliancy.

Aurelia - *Is there anything else you want to share?*

Adama - If it were not for the intervention and the glorious and beautiful new light so generously flooding your planet now from our Creator, the Earth and humanity would soon be facing a different scenario. Your present generation could be wiped out spiritually and the Earth would again experience much destruction and a major setback from her ultimate destiny. This is why there is so much new channeled information being disseminated. Much is on the Internet where many willing and dedicated Lightworkers share free information from the heart to assist others.

> ***There are still those who believe that everyone will ascend, no questions asked, with all their human baggage unresolved.***

Allow me to say that this will certainly not be the case. It is true that everyone will eventually ascend, but it may not be in this lifetime or from this planet. The important message right now for the youth of the world, and those not so young in age as well, I repeat once more:

> ***"Get off the fence or you may have to get off the planet. The time for complacency is now over."***

Accountability cannot be escaped for those forsaking their destiny, tearing their chakras, and diminishing their health and their beautiful light through drug use and other addictive substances (alcohol, cigarettes, etc.). There is still time right now to heal yourself if you choose. Divine Grace is now available through a most magnificent window of opportunity.

The essence of what we all seek is divine love and freedom from pain and suffering. The path to wholeness is much easier when you use self-love as your companion. Thank you for your concern and for your love. It was my great pleasure to commune with you this day. I love you all so very much.

I am Adama, offering you my love, comfort and support.

Chapter Six

The Will of God, A First Ray Activity

Adama with Master El Morya

Adama speaks to us of the Blue Ray/Flame, the Ray of the Will of God. He explains the spiritual benefits of surrender to the Divine Will and offers a wonderful meditation which gives us a greater understanding of the word surrender.

Aurelia Louise

I feel great excitement because I know something big is in the making on the planet. I also know that energy is shifting rapidly now and the veils of separation between dimensions are gradually thinning. The ascended masters are in closer and increasingly personal contact with us, now more than they have been in thousands of years. If I compare how things used to be when I was a child or in my twenties with how they are now, there is a silver lining forming on the horizon. Even if the dark clouds are not yet completely dispelled, everyone is beginning to feel the changes. That is what I would like to share.

As we allow this unfoldment to take place, embracing all the steps, we discover the magic in it. It took a while for me to see and feel it, but now I really do. Those of us working directly with beings from the other side of the veil as teachers, are here to show the way for those seeking to create a better world. Ultimately, our lives are our own journey and no matter how much assistance is offered, no one can conduct our journey for us.

The next ten years will be the most important and crucial years we have ever lived on this planet. They will determine what we will become and where we will go in our cosmic future.

The planet and humanity have now reached the end of a major cosmic cycle. The Earth and those choosing it are now moving into a new cycle of enlightened evolution. As souls evolving on Her body, we are faced with the most important choices we will ever make. We must choose whether or not we want to accompany the Earth into a brand new reality of love and light or stay behind for another long round of incarnations in the third dimension. It is up to us to decide whether we want to experience the new world here or move on to another third dimensional planet in another universe and continue to experience life with the limitations and challenges that third dimensional life offers.

Our Earth deserves Her glorious ascension. The bells of her own graduation to a new cosmic cycle are now ringing. After all, despite the infinite love and tolerance she has offered humanity, she has not received much gratitude in return. She has offered us her body unconditionally, allowing us the opportunity to experiment with free will. The question now is, do we choose to move along to the next level, or do we stay behind? What reality are we really choosing to create and embrace for ourselves in the next few remaining years?

I constantly hear people lament that they are so caught up in everyday living that, as much as they want to do spiritual and healing work for the benefit of their evolution, their true spiritual quest is always put off for another time. They say, "Well, I'll do it tomorrow or next month, or perhaps next year when things are more conducive or when my life slows down a little bit. Then I will have more time for my healing and spiritual work." Do you realize that time waits for no one, and we are now at the threshold of monumental change?

What the Ascended Masters — Adama, Sananda, Maitreya, Archangel Michael, Saint Germain — and all other masters are telling us is that right NOW there is nothing, absolutely nothing, more important than our personal spiritual and healing work. Everything else is a distraction to keep us away from the real goal of our incarnation here.

The positive changes we so long for will only become a reality in our personal lives as a result of that work. Bottom line, there is no other way around it. Nothing will change in our lives unless we change it ourselves; this is our individual responsibility. This is what we came here to do in this life and if we do not want to do it, no one else can do it for us.

Yes, we do have to attend to the many obligations of our daily lives, but ultimately what will really count and make the difference for us in the next few years is not so much what we have done, but what we have become!

Contemplate this: What we do comes and goes in the passage of time, but what we become, as divine beings, embracing our divinity from the perspective of a human experience, remains with us for eternity.

Hmmm.... Adama is here. He is patiently waiting for me to finish talking. Perhaps he is wondering who has been invited to speak here today, him or me. *(Laugh!)*

Adama

Greetings, my beloved friends! I am speaking to you this day from my elegant home in Telos, but I am with all of you at the same time. We have today a silent partner in the awe-inspiring presence of our dear friend El Morya. We both want to convey our deep love to all those connecting with our hearts through this sharing.

Today I would like to talk about the Will of God as the path of "surrender." You see, without the Will of God you will not go very far on your evolutionary pathway. This is the very first step, the first initiation that must be mastered before you can really progress through all the other steps. If you are not willing to surrender to the "greater will" of your being, the Will of your own "Divine Source," how will you find your way home to the realm of Light? If you are not willing to surrender to that which is seeking to bring you all the way back "home," to your divine perfection, joy, bliss and limitlessness, your lost paradise, how do you expect to ever get there?

The Will of God is not a God outside you. It is simply the God that you are and that you have always been, although when in physical incarnation you tend to forget temporarily. Your divine Presence is omniscient, omnipresent and omnipotent and can fulfill all of your desires. You have temporarily forgotten that you are nothing less than an expression of this great I AM, incarnated in a human form. You came here with an agenda to attain soul perfection and expand your own divinity to the fullness of your God-Mastery and Wisdom. You are here seeking advanced enlightenment and total spiritual freedom. You are here to become an unlimited God in all planes of existence. This is an agenda of love for the Self and that Self is no one but "you." You are still too caught up in your mundane affairs, not seeking to attain the goals you established for this incarnation. For too many of you, the affairs of your soul path and soul evolution have become the last concerns on your agenda.

Well, my dear friends, when you consciously put aside the true goals of your incarnation for the sake of momentary human pursuits, your life does not reflect what you envisioned for yourself prior to your incarnation here. Once back on the other side of the veil, as you review the life just completed, there are always deep regrets. There is a profound desire to receive another opportunity for incarnation, to fulfill all the soul's desires in the most recent life. This is how the merry-go-round of endless incarnations for the soul is created, one incarnation after the other. Your divine presence, with great patience and compassion, has granted you thousands upon thousands of these opportunities. For so many of you, each time you came here you ignored the reasons for your coming.

Lifetime after lifetime you did not meet your goals for that incarnation. This is why you are still here facing many challenges instead of enjoying the bliss of the light realms. You will keep coming back, again and again, until you finally surrender to the longings of your own soul. Your Divine Presence has watched you suffer endlessly for many lifetimes. It has observed your pain, your despair, your hopelessness, your fears, your tears, your doubts, your shames and your terrors. It has witnessed the great wisdom that has been gained in all of these incarnations, individually and for the whole of Creation. It is longing now to bring you home, to freedom, to love, to mastery, to oneness, and to all that you are as a divine being.

It yearns to bring you back home, but it cannot force you; it requires your willingness, your intention and your cooperation. It requires that you embrace all parts of yourself that you have abandoned and hated along the way through your many incarnations. Your GodSelf is calling you now to *"surrender"* to the path that is laid before you, day by day, with love and trust. Through that loving surrender, step-by-step, you will be shown the way back to the "sun of your being," your divine perfection.

This is why surrender to the Will of your own divinity bestows such divine grace upon yourself.

It is "you" who will be the great beneficiary of this grace. Someday you will wonder why you have waited so long to finally come "Home." Someday you will realize that you really never had to suffer; it was your choice. It was your resistance to the Love that you are that created all the pain and lessons you have experienced for so long. It is now time to embrace a way of life that will nurture all of you, instead of one that diminishes you.

When you surrender, it is the human ego, also known as the altered ego, that you gradually transform back into the original consciousness of your divine nature. As you surrender to the process of cleansing and healing yourself with absolute trust, without judgment and without fear, you can get through this rather quickly. The process of surrender is much less painful than fighting it all the way. The first step is always the hardest and most overwhelming part of the path. Trust that once you have taken that step, the rest is much easier.

When you resist what is best for your pathway, your soul will simply allow you to have your own way until you can't stand it anymore. Time is not of the essence for the soul, but we, the masters of light, know that all of you have suffered on this planet long enough. We invite you now to choose a more joyful destiny.

In Telos, it is with great interest that we have been watching the reactions of the thousands of people who have read our information in our first book. So many of you, if not all of you, have experienced great heart openings. Your ancient memories have been awakened. We have watched the tears of hope and yearning when you read the material about our lives in Telos and Lemuria. You have become aware that a different kind of life is not only possible on this planet, but is being created by those embracing transformation through self-love and spiritual wisdom. With our assistance, this is what we invite you to do today.

We have already walked the pathway for ourselves, thus opening the way for you to follow in our footsteps, holding our hands out to you. Because we are here for you now, the way will be much easier than it was for us. For all those desiring to join with us and share the lifestyle we enjoy, the path of love and surrender is the key to your homecoming.

> *We have reached the level of divine grace we are experiencing today in our lives only because, a long time ago, we "surrendered" to that divine will. By doing so, our lives were gradually transformed and so will yours be.*

What we had to do, we did under circumstances that were much more difficult and painful than the situations you are presently experiencing. Let me say something about our passage to the Light 12,000 years ago. You might be surprised to know that after the destruction of our continent, all of us had to work out all of our issues in the same manner as is required of you at this time.

Consider that overnight, we lost everything we ever owned, everything we had ever identified with in Lemuria and, most painful of all, we were separated abruptly from nearly everyone we had ever loved. All the beauty of Lemuria, all our work over the ages, all the aspects of our day-to-day lives had suddenly vanished.

> *All that was left was "ourselves," the divine aspect of self that we had to surrender to in order to receive again from our Creator.*

Telos was then in a rather primitive state compared to the glorious and beautiful city it has become. We built a city in a large cave inside the mountain to save the small percentage of our people who survived, and what was left of our culture.

Understand that overnight, we had to adjust our lives to a

lower standard of living that was quite difficult for a long time. With great courage and determination we forged a new life for ourselves. As time passed, we continued to build our city, not only for ourselves, but for future generations who would be born here in the Lemurian culture. Having lost everything except ourselves, we worked very hard for centuries, healing the wounds of our losses and creating something new and more permanent. It would require several volumes to describe all of the difficult challenges we had to face.

Our homecoming a long time ago, my dear friends, was not as simple as you might imagine. You are all on "easy street" at this time compared to the obstacles we had to overcome. We ask you not to be dismayed by what you are going through in your lives, but rather to surrender to the process. Surrender with "willing acceptance" to the events that will take place on your planet. They will come for the purpose of your deliverance from the chains you have created for yourselves. Simply open your heart to love and "trust" that your passage to the Light, as it was with ours, will not manifest without your conscious and sustained effort. Be assured that the rewards will be magnificent for those who persevere.

The Will of God is known as a First Ray activity, and resonates with a blue vibration.

It is like a beautiful peacock-to-royal-blue in color. Its frequency is vibrant, alive and cleansing. It is also connected with what we call "the Diamond Heart." Like any diamond, surrender to this Divine Will has many facets. Archangel Michael is a Blue Ray Angel and Master El Morya is a blue ray master, the guardian of the Diamond Heart of the Will of God.

The Blue Ray is the ray of divine power and leadership, the ray of power through the spoken and silent word. This is why it is connected with the throat chakra. It is the ray that has been most misused by humanity. Each time you are not speaking words of love and compassion you are misusing the energies of this ray. Each time you attempt to control or manipulate in order to have your own way, you are misusing the energies of the blue ray. And be aware, the misuse of this energy is often performed in very subtle ways—so subtle, in fact, that you are not aware of it unless you are able to monitor all thoughts, words and actions from the heart center.

You understand and know what I mean. The Blue Ray will allow you to align in consciousness with the other masters. Master El Morya is known as a spiritual disciplinarian; his discipline is a reflection of the love he holds in his soul for all of you.

The rays are part of the basic curriculum you must master for this phase of your evolution. You have to master the God attributes of all seven rays equally, as well as the five secret rays. There is not one ray more important, greater or lesser, than the others. They need to be mastered, balanced and equally understood.

In different lifetimes, you may not always be working on the same ray. You are endeavoring to integrate and gain the wisdom of all of the rays. You were originally created on one of the rays, and this ray remains your permanent one. It is also called the monadic ray. However, because you originate as a blue or yellow or green ray soul it does not mean that you will work with that ray in every lifetime. You usually strive to gain mastery with two rays, and balance the others in oneness. You do this until you have mastered and balanced all the ray energies at deeper and deeper levels and passed all required initiations for ascension.

People come to the Earth plane for the very purpose of forging their spiritual mastery.

Diligent work brings this about. This is why you have chosen to incarnate so many times. You cannot expect to gain full mastery of the divine by simply wishing it to be so. It does not work that way. The perfection and refinement of the soul is accomplished through a series of incarnations in the third dimension. For those of you who live with the illusion that space brothers are going to come rescue you from doing spiritual work to evolve your consciousness, you are setting yourself up for a big disappointment. For those of you imagining that you are simply going to be taken unconditionally into the light realm, I say, revise your thinking. The space brothers are not allowed to come and rescue you. There is no need for rescue because you have created the lifetime you are now living for the explicit purpose of soul growth.

> *In every lifetime, you incarnate on Earth*
> *through a personal choice you make. You*
> *have never been forced to come back here.*

You choose in each and every lifetime the goals and experiences of your incarnation for the purpose of evolving your soul consciousness and gaining greater mastery. When you are on the other side between incarnations and become aware of all you have left undone during the last incarnation, you choose to come back. Your real desire is to align with and fulfill all your goals. You ask for another opportunity, and another, again and again, until you feel you have completed this phase of your evolution.

Each time you arrive here in the physical body, the veil of forgetfulness drops again and you feel trapped and cut off, totally immersed in the illusion. Life on this planet has been difficult for humanity because the consciousness has dropped to such a level of density, distortion and separation from divine principles. Humanity has gone as far as it can go into separation. The lessons learned, the experience gathered and the knowledge acquired are all invaluable.

This is now gradually shifting through the unprecedented assistance from the light realms and the civilizations of the Earth's interior. Separation in the third dimension was an experiment to understand how souls would react when totally cut off from God. All of you in physical bodies volunteered for this cosmic project; otherwise you would not be here.

This great experiment, in which you so excitedly volunteered to participate millions of years ago, had a beginning time frame and an ending one. It has assisted the people of Earth to become strong and courageous souls. Because of their great sacrifices, the souls of Earth are now being lifted into greater glory, forging for themselves a grand destiny. You will become the showcase of this universe and the teachers of new civilizations to be born.

As you align yourselves with the Will of God through surrender, you are destined to become among the most "in-demand" souls anywhere in this and other universes. Planet Earth, which has experienced such great darkness and pain, will soon be lifted into a state of love and light, a way-shower for others. In truth, there is really no other place like Earth. Be proud and hopeful to be a citizen of this planet. You have suffered long enough, and it is now time for all of you to come home. It is with such wondrous anticipation that we wait to greet you and to hold you in our arms. We long to welcome you back to the valley of love, where the valley of tears has become the valley of joy.

As you peel off the layers of hurt and trauma from the past, many of you discover that you have a lack of trust in God and Spirit. For you, "surrender" to divine will is a fearful proposal.

You feel that you have been betrayed and abandoned in this and other lifetimes. This core issue has been part of the original fall in consciousness. The original separation from your Divine Source created pain. Pain then created the world in which you now live. Separation allowed for the manifestations of individuation necessary to create the experiences you have had on this planet. How can you truly know God and your Self, without knowing what it is to not know God? What first began as a little fear and doubt grew into a lack of trust in God and yourselves.

Your test now is to allow yourself to trust the divine again and heal the consciousness that has created the separation from God. The universe is a loving and a benevolent place and will provide you with everything when you "trust." "The fall" gradually evolved as a few incarnated souls began questioning whether God was always going to provide. After several million years when the Creator provided everything for everyone without fail, some began to contemplate what might happen if the supply suddenly stopped. They allowed themselves to "fall into the consciousness" that without God providing, they would have to provide for themselves. This distorted concept, held at first by only a few, was eventually communicated to the masses.

The fears that gave birth to this lack of trust became more and more amplified, enveloping the whole human race. They almost gave up their divine birthright, and the rest is history.

Surrender to God's Will presents to the soul the initiations and the opportunity to restore the divine birthright. This lack of trust is what must be healed now. To do so takes courage and commitment. Stepping off the dock of what is known into the deep still waters of the unknown is the ultimate act of trust. Allow your heart to hear the call of your soul and you will know what choice to make. You will know what your true purpose is on this planet at this time of acceleration and evolution.

When you chose to "not trust," God allowed you the experience and the many consequences as well as the wisdom that eventually came from it.

The fear people feel in trusting God is in making a commitment to the Higher Self to achieve their mastery and ascension and return home. This requires that you clear all issues. In the process, your Higher Self brings into your experience all the shadow material you have created for yourself throughout the ages. These issues must be examined in order to have the opportunity of making new choices in love and trust, rather than in fear.

All issues needing to be balanced and understood and any residual karma needing to be cleared are brought to your attention. Facing all of this can be temporarily challenging. You may think, "I made a commitment to start trusting God and my life has become more challenging." Then you may choose to fall back into the cycle of mistrust. The path is to allow whatever is presented to you, and to witness it even if it is difficult for a while. No matter what appears in your life, even if it becomes temporarily more difficult, trust that you are on a new road and that the energy will eventually shift. Regardless of the millions of years of mistrust you have expressed toward your Creator, this homecoming to your true self can manifest rather quickly.

Think of Job in your scriptures. He was severely tested, but he continued to trust. When he was able to prove to God that he would continue to trust, in spite of everything he had lost, including his health and his wife and children, all was restored to him and much more. First, he had to journey through the dark night of the soul and so will you!

Allow yourself the process of going through this dark night. Finally, face all that you have hidden in the shadows for so long, without any judgment or attachment. It is in these shadows that you will also find all of your gifts. You will rediscover the attributes of your divine birthright, and your full energies will be restored to you. You will once again trust your Creator and your surrender in total love will be your rescue, not your despair.

All of humanity is basically experiencing the same path of evolution. There is no need for shame or regret because all of you have the same issues. Your current experience may look different, but it is shared by everyone. Lack of trust and a separation from your Source have created this long, long journey of suffering. Now is the time to resurrect yourself fully through love and trust.

When you can finally say, "I will let go of my misconceptions and fears and trust the process, no matter how painful it gets," you will have taken the hardest step. When you finally face your heartbreak and anger, it is not quite as painful as you expected. The process, if allowed, will take you all the way "home" and you will finally experience the end of all suffering and lack. You will understand the universe and your life with a new level of compassion and acceptance. The struggle that has ruled your life will abate.

> ***Once you have conquered that fear,***
> ***everything is open to you and you can***
> ***have everything without limitation.***

Nothing is withheld from you anymore. You will know with absolute certainty that this universe you have feared for so long will provide everything you ever wanted and everything you ever needed. What you call original sin, which I call the original breach of confidence with God, is basically the last thing you need to conquer. That correlates with the Adam and Eve story, which is a metaphor to describe the lack of trust in God, which led to separation.

Yes, Adam and Eve is just a story recorded with little understanding. Though the allegory in your scriptures may contain some levels of truth, it certainly did not happen that way. The story of Adam and Eve and the fall from grace of humanity is very complex indeed. Some day all the true records will be made available to humanity and you will finally understand and learn much from it. That story is simply an inaccurate representation of what actually happened.

People stopped trusting in their Creator and went into fear. Aurelia has among her possessions a little book called *The Sons of God,* by Christine Mercer. This is the story of a woman who decided to trust God, no matter what happened to her. Her trust was put to the most extreme tests. She made a determined and heartfelt decision to never, ever again complain about anything. She continued trusting, no matter how painful it became. Even though she made this deep commitment to her "surrender," she was most severely tested. The happy ending of this true story is that in a short time, she balanced such a tremendous amount of karma that miracles upon miracles began to flow in her life. All she had lost was restored a hundred-fold.

During the testing period she thanked God for every difficulty she was experiencing, knowing that this was going to lead her to something much greater, and it certainly did! She was eventually able to take her body into physical ascension a few years later. At that time, the energies on the planet did not yet support such an activity, as they do today.

This little book made a big impression on Aurelia when she was going through a rather difficult time herself. She read late into the night, from cover to cover, this book she found for $2.00 in a used bookstore. Aurelia's reaction was, "... Hmmm. I guess my situation, which is by no means as severe as hers, could possibly be improved by using the same principles she did." She reflected in her heart that her attitude toward her life situation was far from graceful or grateful, and that she was harboring resentment.

She read the book twice and then decided to apply the principles in "an attitude of gratitude" as best she could. Aurelia's situation improved almost immediately, and within a few months she was again happier than she had been in a long time. Her heart was free and her financial situation was restored.

Christine's book is worth its weight in gold. The way this woman conquered her fears, for herself and in her life, is a great example for everyone to follow.

I would like to explain the purpose of being tested.

Understand that God does not test you just to be malicious. When you open yourself to that surrender for the sake of regaining your spiritual freedom, you are not experiencing an outside force trying to make you uncomfortable. The testing is an opportunity you have invited to clear and balance the negativity you have created in the past. When you choose to heal for your spiritual growth, your I AM Presence will provide the experiences that allow this healing to take place.

When you put yourself into a state of total trust, the universe responds and begins providing immediately.

God does not really want to test you. God is Love and His Love is unconditional. When you open yourself to the surrender we are talking about, the universe will provide all the situations and opportunities needed to balance your issues and heal them forever. In great amazement, you will discover how quickly the universe responds to your requests when you are aligned with Divine Will.

I want to express one more thing before the meditation. The minute you make a true and consistent commitment to your God Presence to totally surrender yourself to the process of change and transformation, your Presence will guide you to the fastest and smoothest way to obtain the object of your desires and to open the "Door of Everything."

Opening to the will of God is done through surrender. The

will of God is the very attribute that will take you all the way home to grace. Souls on this planet need to realize that before they can go to specific masters for initiations and advancement, they must first pass the tests of El Morya, the tests of surrender to the Divine Will. When you decide to make a real commitment to your ascension and to your spiritual journey, if you are not willing to pass the tests of surrender, how will you pass the other tests? Other masters may not be able to work with you until you have understood the various aspects of the Blue Ray. Then, when you have made yourself ready for another master, you are gracefully escorted there with a "recommendation."

I have been looking forward to giving you this talk about surrender. This is what is most needed at the present time. Going beyond fear is the key. As more and more people let go of their fear, it will become easier for others to do so. If you want to know how you can assist this planet, the most important thing you can do is let go of your own fears. Surrender with Love to what is and let go of all judgment. The more you practice this and encourage others to do the same, the smoother will be the pathway you create for yourself and for the rest of humanity. You can best serve your planet by clearing yourself first.

Meditation

Journey to the Will of God Temple in Telos

We have in Telos a temple consecrated to the Will of God. There is also such a temple in Darjeeling, India, near Tibet. The retreat of the Will of God is under the guardianship of the master El Morya, both in Darjeeling and Mount Shasta. Many of you go there at night or come here to Telos to learn the initiations of the First Ray, of surrender to Divine Will. Darjeeling is the original temple for the Will of God and it existed long before we built ours in Telos. They both exist in the fifth dimension frequency, and thus are not visible to you. Today, I would like to take you in consciousness to our Will of God temple in Telos.

I ask that you focus in your heart and take several deep breaths. Consciously ask your divine Presence or your higher self to take you on a journey with us to Telos.

See yourself arriving here in your personal merkaba, accompanied by one of your guides. Notice a fairly large opalescent blue structure, quite tall, in the form of a six-sided pyramid. As you approach, everything around you resonates with the beautiful blue energy, so refreshing and soothing. Allow yourself to walk up the mother-of-pearl stairway to the main entrance of the temple. Observe and feel the majestic blue mist emanating from various high fountains all around it. Many varieties of blue flowers growing in white and gold boxes flourish in great abundance around the fountains, including the sweet forget-me-nots. Walk now through the entrance, where three Blue Flame angels are waiting to escort and welcome you.

As you enter the large hallway, see a transparent chamber in the center containing a huge Blue Flame diamond, the biggest diamond that you will ever see, about 15 to 18 feet in height. Your guide invites you to enter that sacred chamber. The diamond contains several thousand facets, each one representing a different aspect of that Diamond Heart of the Divine Will. This diamond is not so different from the one living within your heart, and in time all the wondrous facets of your own diamond heart will become completely activated and restored. Your Diamond Heart and your sacred heart are one and the same; they are components of each other. They are made of an infinite number of chambers, each one corresponding to a facet of your own diamond.

As you come into the sacred chamber of the Divine Will, you are greeted by master El Morya, a tall being with brown eyes who looks very much like a Zen master. He is wearing a blue robe partially covered by a luminescent white cape, with a bluish white and gold turban on his head. He greets and welcomes you to His Diamond Heart, and invites you to find a seat on one of the "blue-flame" cushions. He guides you to focus on the energy of that diamond heart and to breathe in the energies so that you may bring as much of this energy as possible back with you when you return to your physical body. This Blue Ray is the one that gives the power to the Love Ray. All the rays contain love plus the specific attributes of each ray.

In the presence of this diamond you can open all the facets of your own diamond heart that are full of fears, and let them go. Allow the energies of this huge diamond to magnetize and absorb your fears, dear ones, and let them be released and healed. As you release these fears from your heart, you will receive a tremendous healing.

Be aware that it may be difficult to release all your fears and burdens in one visit. This is why we invite you to return to this temple in Telos or in Darjeeling as often as you wish to receive deeper levels of healing. Inner healing is an ongoing process until you reach completion. Consider your efforts as a work in progress, and be willing to stay with the process until all the veils are lifted. Then you will know you are complete.

Now connect with your higher self right above you. Your great I AM Presence, the unlimited being that is really who you are, is waiting for all your fears to be released and healed. Connect with this Divine presence, and if you feel ready, make your commitment to surrender all the fears that have kept you in so much pain, so you can be restored to wholeness.

No matter what may show up in your life tomorrow, it is only a mirror of a fear or old pattern of belief held within yourself that still needs to be resolved and embraced. You will soon come to know, as you do this work, that there is nothing to fear except the illusion of fear itself.

Keep breathing in this wonderful blue flame right into your lungs and heart. Do this consciously because you want to bring this energy back into your physical body. Know that all your multi-dimensional aspects and all the beings of the light realms are supporting your journey home to Divine Grace. You are not alone in your journey; you have so much love and support available to you. You can do it if you choose to.

Feel the soothing action of the blue flame. It has its own way of bringing you comfort and easing all your pain.

Now Master El Morya and I have a gift for each one of you sitting in front of the diamond in our temple. We are going to superimpose a smaller etheric diamond of total perfection, radiating the qualities of the blue-essence, within the energies of your own sacred heart chamber.

This diamond will reflect to you the divine perfection of the diamond heart you are striving to acquire. With this gift, the perfection of the Diamond Heart will be reflected to you constantly, as long as you choose to work with it. We invite you to begin breathing in its energies every day in your meditation. Work with these energies in any way that seems appropriate for you. In your meditation, ask your higher self to show you which facets of the diamond still hold pain or unbalanced attitudes that need to be healed and re-aligned. The diamond you have just received will continue to reflect everything you need for the complete opening and healing of your heart. It will take you to the path of surrender with joy and grace. It is alive and vibrant. Its color reflects a luminescent peacock blue.

Keep breathing its energies with allowance and surrender to what is. Be resolute in walking this path and feel free to communicate with your guide. Stay with this energy and be thankful for the grace you have just received. *(Pause)*

When you feel complete, return to your body, taking this treasure with you. The more you remain conscious and work with the Diamond Heart, the more its energies will amplify and bless your life. This is a gift or tool we give to you, but it will not help you unless you use it. Remember, what you don't use, you lose. This Diamond Heart also carries the vibration of self-confidence. Tap into this energy to assist in releasing your fears so that your surrender can be accomplished gracefully.

All the Blue Ray masters are available to you at this time, offering their assistance. When you feel ready, open your eyes. We invite you to return to this healing place often, to meditate with us on the Will of God and to continue to seek your spiritual freedom. And so be it, Beloved I AM.

The world would seem
A much darker place,
If the light of our love for each other,
And the Divine,
Did not flood every step of our path.
- Ahnahmar

Chapter Seven

The Violet Flame of Freedom and Transmutation A Seventh Ray Activity

Adama and Master Saint Germain

Adama speaks to us about the Violet Ray, the Ray of Transmutation, accompanied by Master Saint Germain. A wonderful meditation is offered instructing us in how to use the Violet Flame on our personal path to mastery.

Aurelia - The Violet Ray resonates with the energy of change, alchemy and freedom. I wish now to invite you to open yourself to heart-to-heart communion with Adama and Master Saint Germain. Adama is quite the heart doctor, as is Saint Germain. As he speaks, Adama addresses your heart directly, activating its healing power. This is something Adama likes to do. He is the one who can help you embrace the higher vibrations of Telos.

Group - *Could you explain who Saint Germain is for those not familiar with this alchemical master?*

Aurelia - Master Saint Germain is and has been for eons of time the guardian of the Violet Flame. Within the Spiritual Hierarchy, he holds the position of the Chohan of the Seventh Ray. This means that he is the guardian of the Violet Flame of Freedom and Transmutation for the planet.

In one of his many previous incarnations he was Joseph, the father of Master Jesus, who lived 2,000 years ago. He also incarnated as the prophet Samuel, Christopher Columbus and Francis Bacon, the true author of the Shakespearian plays. He was asked once why he gave the plays to Shakespeare instead of taking the credit for himself, and he replied, "Karma balancing."

Last, but not least, he was very well known in France, prior to and during the French revolution, as "The Count of Saint Germain." This immortal being lived and was seen regularly by many for over 300 years, always maintaining the appearance of a 40-year-old man. He was called "The Wonder Man of Europe," who spoke all languages, played any and all musical instruments and demonstrated, in front of his friends, many activities of alchemy. He was known for his ability to materialize in one place, dematerialize in a few moments and reappear several hundred miles away a few minutes later. He has a wonderful sense of humor and is exceptionally articulate in words, especially in the English language. Saint Germain has always been a real delight to my soul whenever I have had contact with this beloved one. To hear or mention his name makes my heart sing with gladness.

The great Master Saint Germain is the one who has kept the Flame of Freedom alive for the planet for over 70,000 years. He is an awe-inspiring and beloved master. As Master Jesus was the great Hierarch of the Piscean age, Saint Germain is now stepping in, for the next 2,000 years, as the great Hierarch of the Aquarian age. He is fully supported by Jesus/Sananda and our Lemurian family of Telos, as well as the spiritual hierarchy of this planet and this galaxy and universe. Some masters hold certain offices for a length of time and then move on to another post. Their former post is filled by someone at that level of attainment willing to be trained for new planetary service.

Group - Was he also embodied as the great Merlin of Camelot?

Aurelia - Oh, yes, he was Merlin in the time of Camelot in England. Merlin was a noble magician, a great master alchemist. Unfortunately, he has been depicted in many books and movies as a wizard of some kind, with a dubious reputation. That is not the truth of who Merlin was. In truth, he was one of the greatest alchemists of all times, and one of the greatest masters in service to this planet since its inception.

All other masters honor him greatly for the service he has rendered humanity by maintaining the Violet Flame. The Violet Flame is one of the most important flames for redemption, transmutation and freedom. It is like a fire of love that cleanses. Saint Germain said once that if he were to talk about the Violet Flame for a whole month, 24 hours a day, 7 days a week, he could not cover all its benefits. Let's hear what Adama has to say.

Adama - Good evening my beloved friends, this is Adama of Telos. Tonight, as always, I have my regular team of twelve masters with me. We enjoy the great pleasure of having Master Saint Germain present with us as a participant. Although I am talking through Aurelia, the energy of Saint Germain is blended with mine. This is such an honor for us, because Master Saint Germain is so deeply loved on the inner planes and so highly respected by everyone throughout the entire cosmos. He spends a great deal of time with us in Telos, as we all work together to bring forth the energies of ascension for the planet and for humanity.

I would like to begin by giving you some explanation about the Seventh Ray. If you have questions, feel free to interrupt so we can create more of a dialogue.

The Violet Flame is a combination of the blue and pink rays; it is not one ray by itself, but a combination of blue for power and pink for love, uniting the energies of the divine masculine with the divine feminine through the action of spiritual alchemy. The primary role of the Violet Flame is transmutation, an alchemical term meaning to create positive change. For example, by invoking and working with the Violet Flame you can transmute karma or misqualified energy from this or past lifetimes into pure positive energy. As you lovingly invoke, with intention, the attributes of the Violet Fire, the energy is transmuted. You never have to deal with it anymore in your present life because these energies have been erased and forgiven into love and joy. As you work with this energy with the love and fires of your heart, the Violet Consuming Flame dissipates and dissolves unbalanced energies in your subtle bodies. It can heal the many conditions in your lives needing re-alignment.

The Violet Flame can dissolve karma once you fully understand your past experiences and the energy patterns you created. With its energies you can also create wondrous beauty because it is composed of power and love energies. Also included in the Violet Ray activity is the flame of forgiveness and compassion, which are relevant to creating harmony and manifestation in your life.

Other attributes of the Violet Flame include the energies of comfort, of diplomacy and of ceremonies. These are all Seventh Ray activities. Whenever you create comfort, no matter what form it takes, you engage in a Seventh Ray activity. We also call the Violet Flame the Freedom Love Flame. What kind of freedom are we talking about? We speak of spiritual freedom. When you gain spiritual freedom you become limitless and all attributes of your divinity are at your command. This is the kind of freedom you all yearn for; total freedom. The Violet Flame is a vital tool for your spiritual progress and evolution.

Aurelia - What exactly do you mean when you talk about the process of spiritual awakening? How can we begin to use the Violet Flame to heal ourselves and to heal our lives?

Adama - The Seventh Ray can assist in the purification

of the substances and the energies of life. There are many ways you can use the Violet Flame constructively and effectively. You can use it in your prayers, invocations and meditations. In your meditations, you can visualize yourself receiving an infusion of this energy throughout all aspects of your being.

Breathe it into every cell, atom and electron of your body. Allow it to cleanse and purify every thought and feeling in your auric field and your subtle bodies. Be creative and begin formulating your own prayers and invocations to the Violet Flame. When these come from the fire of your own heart they are more powerful than those written by others. Prayers written by others can be useful, but they are more suited to those who wrote them. Work with it each day and begin creating miracles of love in your lives.

Invocation to the Violet Flame

As an example, *"In the name of the I AM of my being, in the name of God, I now call forth the action of the Violet Flame of transmutation, compassion and forgiveness in my auric field, for the cleansing and purifying of every thought and feeling in my solar plexus and in all of my chakras. I ask the action of the Violet Fire to permeate every cell, atom and electron of my four body systems at this moment and at all times each day of my life, 24 hours a day, 7 days a week, for the healing of all distortions in my energy fields from past and present misunderstandings. I ask the energies of the Violet Fire to heal all distortions in my physical, emotional and mental bodies. With much gratitude, I now ask for the action of the Violet Fire to manifest in my energy fields in full power. And so be it."*

You can use this kind of invocation and create your own as well. Sit quietly as you visualize and breathe it in. Using the breath in a conscious and sustained manner brings it into your auric field in a more tangible and creative manner.

Then you can ask the Violet Flame to sustain this activity for the rest of the day and it will continue its action while you perform your other activities. The action will continue uninterrupted as long as you remain in harmony. Whenever you invoke any flame of God and you ask for its momentum to be sustained, its activity will continue until you engage in disharmony in your feeling world. That vibration stops it; when you make peace within yourself, invoke it again. As long as you stay harmonious in your thoughts and feelings, the flame will continue to work. If you find yourself in disharmony, invoke it again to assist your return to emotional balance.

The more you visualize it, while staying in your heart during your meditation, the more action is building. There was a time with earlier dispensations in the last century when people were not very willing to meditate. So we formulated a series of decrees through which people invoked the Violet Flame or the flame of other rays daily, sometimes for hours and hours. Unfortunately, for many people, this type of devotion became a mental ritual, lacking the real fervor of their hearts.

Though these people meant well and were sincere, it is best to say a decree or prayer only once with all the fervor that the heart can muster, taking the time needed to create the alchemy of love. When you make an invocation or prayer, allow yourself to feel fully its energy in your heart and charge it with love; then allow the energy to do its perfect work.

There are several thousand people in the last century who ascended by invoking the Violet Flame every day for years and years. They invoked it with much love and fervor in their hearts without ever really knowing for sure what they were transmuting. They allowed all their shadows to surface into their awareness, without judgment, and transmuted the energies by bathing them in the Violet Fire. These dear souls did not have access to all the tools and information you have at this time. For them, through faith and consistency they continued until they breathed their last human breath. By this gradual process they changed all the negative energy from many lives, past and present, into pure golden liquid light. When they passed on to the other side of the veil they made their glorious ascension without delay. Today they are among us, wearing robes of Light and enjoying all the glory of the fifth dimension.

Aurelia - Do we have to be consciously aware of what we are transmuting?

Adama - It is good to know in some cases, but it is not always a requirement, as long as you pour your love into it. It is always the love, the forgiveness and the compassion poured into a situation that transmutes it into something better, by changing a negative situation into a positive one and by gaining the wisdom these energies have to teach. If you have a problem with someone, send waves and waves of Violet Flame to him or her. As you send waves of love, compassion, forgiveness and blessing to a situation, it becomes impossible for it to remain the same. Universal law requires resolution for whatever receives love and blessings.

The activity of blessing is also a form of transmutation, a Seventh Ray activity.

As you begin blessing all that manifests as less than divine perfection in your lives, you are transforming or transmuting situations that appear to be negative into something far more positive. You create the divine solution and the win-win situation for everyone eventually manifests, for this is what transmutation does. It creates a transformation that makes everyone a winner.

Aurelia - How would someone having a problem with a spouse or boss or friend use the Violet Flame to transmute or heal their ill feelings?

Adama - First of all, remember that you have to be detached from the outcome. If you desire to make changes or bring about a specific outcome you may not be successful. This is why it is always more appropriate to ask for the perfect divine solution. If you desire to be specific about the outcome you wish to create, it is important that you "allow" a different outcome to manifest by adding to your prayer or intention, "this or something better, according to divine will." Your Higher Self sees and knows the bigger picture that is veiled from you. Let's say a marriage situation appears to be ending. At the time you say, "Oh, my gosh! I prayed and I invoked the Violet Flame for that situation. I did all I could to be loving, compassionate and bring resolution with love and forgiveness, and now it seems I have a more challenging situation."

Now contemplate this: ask yourself if the ending of a marriage is a failure or a spiritual victory. I say that if you have done your very best and a situation does not end the way it was hoped, perhaps it was a karmic relationship that had reached completion. Perhaps your Higher Self is now ready to open your life to something much more appropriate for your happiness. The marriage was certainly a spiritual success, not a failure. Because of the quality of inner work done, the right to move on to something more fulfilling has been earned. The feeling of the loss or sense of failure is but a temporary human illusion.

Two years later, you find yourself in a wondrous new relationship in which you are so much happier and there is much more affinity and harmony. Will you remember then the pool of Violet Fire you previously invoked to create this new avenue in your life? There are times when karmic situations are resolved and it's time to move on. This is the way your prayers are answered. You are now "free" to experience something better versus staying in a relationship that has reached completion. Many times it is important to let go of situations that no longer serve you. The divine solution may not always, at first, appear to be what you want, but whatever is created will always be for your spiritual advancement and will bring the best result. The Violet Flame is also known as the "miracle worker."

When you bless the person you have a problem with, let's say a spouse, a neighbor, your boss, someone in your work environment or a relative, visualize her/him bathing in the Violet Flame of love and transmutation. Desire for that person to become free of his/her own burdens and awaken to their full potential. Do this with compassion and forgiveness. Use the flame of diplomacy in all your interactions with others. This is all part of the Seventh Ray activity. If you begin using the Seventh Ray with its many attributes and have no personal agenda other than wanting the best outcome in alignment with divine will, you will be amazed at the miracles that can manifest in your life and in the lives of others around you. This is how peace on Earth will be created.

Aurelia - I know many people are going to find the part about not having a personal agenda difficult because they also want it their own way.

Adama - Most of you are so focused on the end result of what you want that you tend to lose sight of what you have to release in order to let go and let the God within do its perfect work. All the various flames of God contain divine intelligence and consciousness. They are aware of the bigger picture and they know what is best for you. There are guardians, literally hundreds of thousands of masters, working with each flame.

Wanting it your way is like saying: "Well God, I want this, but I want it my way, even if it is ultimately not for my greatest good." If you insist, don't be surprised if you receive what you asked for. God always wants to give you the desires of your heart, and you may soon realize this is not what you needed. These flames bring forth the most magnificent outcomes in your life, but if you are determined to have it your way, your way will often manifest. When you are so determined to have it your own way, you may discover later that you missed something much better.

We see this happening all the time on the planet. People are very afraid to let go of their personal agendas and allow the wisdom of their higher selves to come forward. They are afraid to trust God or the masters. They have become comfortable in trusting the misaligned human ego instead of a higher intelligence.

Remember, lack of trust was the energy of the original fall of consciousness of mankind. Your experiences with that lack of trust have been very painful, indeed. The need to always be in charge, instead of being "in allowance" has created much disharmony. The higher aspect of "You" loves you totally and wants nothing but your happiness, enlightenment and mastery. This higher aspect of "You" knows exactly how to bring into your life the initiations and circumstances that will open wide the "Door of Everything." Your constant resistance to clearing your fears from your path has created blinders that stop you from perceiving that wondrous doorway that has been available to you all along. Even if you have to go through many dark nights of the soul, surrender to the Divine Will, my beloved friends. Let go of fear and trust the process.

People are afraid to experience the dark night of their own creation. What got people in trouble in the first place was this lack of trust. When people decided that they no longer wished to trust God to feed them three times a day, and decided to get their own food instead, a misalignment was created. When they stopped listening to the voice of their own spirit, they separated themselves from the flow of the Divine. Now, several thousand lifetimes later, there is no trust in the union between Divine Spirit and Will, and nearly everyone lives in fear and lack of some kind. Now is your time, through experience and acceptance, to regain and relearn that energy of trust, in spite of appearances. Through intention and release, through allowance of all that is, the "obstacles" you created which block the access to the "Door of Everything" will be dissolved, and you will be free to "step in." You will finally be home!

Aurelia - Is this the "bottom line" with respect to the healing that needs to take place in all our hearts and souls?

Adama - Exactly. Soon humanity is going to learn their lessons in much more dramatic ways. Events will transpire on this planet and people will have to make choices, the most important choices of many lifetimes. Your Earth Mother will soon no longer tolerate the type of separation that has transpired here. People will have to shape up or ship out. The new world order for this planet is not what your world leaders are projecting. Your Creator has projected instead a life of union with the GodSelf, with Earth and with all Life. Divine order will be soon restored.

Events that appear to be unjust or unfair are usually mirrors of the consciousness of the people involved. They are always created with the energies of the collective consciousness. For example, in your country many people do not like your government; they don't want to become involved in any political activity because it is perceived as too negative. You have many books and websites describing all the wrongs and corruption of your government.

Although what is written and presented to the public is usually true, as your government is corrupt to the very core, you need to remember that your government always mirrors the "consciousness" of the people. When the people collectively raise their consciousness into higher integrity, they no longer attract the kind of government you now have. This is not only for the U.S., but applies to most countries on the planet. When a cataclysm occurs, the same is true. Cataclysms are nothing more than nature's way of cleansing the imbalance or toxicity created by the consciousness of the collective. You do not honor the Earth. You trash her body, create pollution and use her resources unwisely. In so doing, you create large pools of unbalanced energies that must be released and cleansed through these cataclysms sooner or later.

When these balancing cataclysms manifest, they are charged with wave upon wave of Violet Flame, full of God's purifying fire. War balances a tremendous amount of personal and planetary karma. Greater understanding is achieved. It may not seem apparent to those who still strive to control your free will. True, many people have suffered, but they also rebalanced their own personal karma in the process. After World War II, when so much karma was balanced on the planet, it opened the way to the expansion of new technology and the greater ease you enjoy today. Although life may still be difficult for many of you, it is easier than it has been for thousands of years.

Aurelia - Do you mean that everything we experience in our most personal relationships, as a society, as a culture and as a country are all mirrors created to reflect self and the collective consciousness?

Adama - Everything that happens, be it on a personal or global level, whether it is a volcano erupting, an earthquake, a riot or a war, always reflects the unbalanced or repressed energy people hold within themselves. It reflects the anger, fear, deception, greed, human injustice and other grief that people hold within their souls. They are all mirrors, nothing more than mirrors of what is out of alignment at the personal level.

Aurelia - Most people do not understand how we create our reality. They say that if they created their own reality, they would create the perfect body, house, mate, and abundant money, etc.

Adama - The problem is that people have not yet understood or realized how they create. Also, their creation does not necessarily come from this lifetime alone, and "karma" or lack of understanding has to be cleared before a new way can be manifested. People create constantly through their moment-by-moment thoughts and feelings, their words and actions, and the internal dialogue they conduct within their mind during waking hours. People may say, they want the perfect body or marriage, but the thoughts and feelings they entertain most of the time do not support their desires. If someone were to show them, moment-by-moment, what their thoughts and feelings have been, and how unbalanced they are, they would understand why they do not have the healthy body they desire, or the relationship or abundance they want.

To create the reality you want, you must become conscious of your thoughts, feelings, words and actions. Words are very powerful, and they constantly reinforce the energy of your feelings. Yet words do not always match your feelings. You may say, "I want more money," but inside you feel poor. You want to be involved in a better relationship, but inside you feel you do not deserve it and you are not willing to weed out the garden of your soul in order to attract that perfect mate. You say, "I want a perfect body," but inside you do not love yourself. You do not love your body as it is, and you are not in acceptance of the lessons you are learning with your body in its present form.

The body thrives on love, but nearly all of you do not love or take proper care of that body like we do in Telos. Very few of you love yourself enough to nurture yourself and your body properly or consistently. Most of you do not give your body the proper nourishment it needs to rejuvenate and radiate perfect health. How then do you expect to create a perfect body for yourself? You are constantly reaffirming what you do not want.

You live in a house of mirrors and the universe gives you back what you create through your thoughts, feelings and words. When you decree "I'm sick and tired of this or that," you create very powerful affirmations that return the energies you just named. You constantly create affirmations of what you do not want. Be consciously aware that the universe hears you and honors what you say. "If she says she's sick and tired, and keeps affirming it with so much strength and power, it must be what she wants. Let's give it to her or him." So you get the opposite of what you say you want. The mirrors keep reflecting.

Aurelia - Now in terms of using the Violet Flame to balance karma, how do we learn the lesson if we use the Violet Flame to get rid of it?

Adama - The Violet Flame will not "get rid of" karma. That is not its purpose. The Violet Flame will assist in balancing it as well as teach the lessons you need to learn in a more gentle way. If you resist the lessons and understanding your challenging situations teach you, the use of the Violet Flame may not bring the desired results. It cannot be misused to prevent you from the experience and gaining the wisdom that ultimately are the true meaning of karma.

There is a big difference between learning a lesson in a gentle way by heeding your inner guidance, or learning through a painful experience to receive the same understanding. Do you see the difference? The Violet Flame provides a more loving and gentle way of learning lessons with ease and grace. Lessons do not have to be as painful or difficult as most of you are experiencing at this time. Your resistance in opening yourself to higher ways creates the harshness in your lives. In fact, all the Flames and their individual attributes can assist you.

Another Invocation to the Violet Flame

Here is another way to use the Violet Flame as an invocation for the world around you: *"In the name of the great I AM, I call to beloved Saint Germain, the guardian of the Violet Flame, to saturate the world with waves upon waves of Violet Fire, to infuse every particle of life, every man, woman and child on this planet in an auric field of Violet Flame to protect and to awaken them. I ask that this action be sustained until perfection is restored. And so be it."*

You may invoke this in your daily prayers and call on the millions of Violet Flame angels that are waiting to go to work. Send them everywhere in the world and fill the world with Violet Fire. Understand that angels are not allowed to interfere in your world unless the call comes from your plane. Send them to work; they are waiting to answer your request. Violet Flame angels can literally flood the planet with Violet Fire and diminish much pain. In your daily life, ask them to flood your personal world with Violet Flame energy. Many forest fires have been stopped because a few people invoked the Violet Flame to intercede.

Aurelia - *It seems important to send the energy of the flame out to every man, woman and child on the planet, and through our hearts, flood the Earth with this energy.*

Adama - Yes, and don't forget the animals, the trees, the elementals, the nature spirits and the plant kingdom. The elementals are very often in need of your assistance, your love, your support and your invocations to the Violet Flame to be able to maintain balance on the planet. They need it now more than ever during this time of transition. The elementals are very involved in assisting the evolution of the planet into a higher octave. They are your helpers. The more Violet Flame and the more love they receive from humanity, the smoother the transitions are going to be for the Earth herself and for all kingdoms living on her body.

Aurelia - Adama, do the Lemurians use the Violet Flame in Telos to maintain the level of perfection you all experience there?

Adama - You bet we do. We use the energies of the Violet Flame constantly. In various temples in Telos, the energies of the sacred fires are perpetually invoked by the members of the priesthood and by many volunteers as well. In our main temple, the temple of Ma-Ra, we have an area consecrated to each one of the main sacred flames. Our people take turns tending and nurturing these flames around the clock. We live in the consciousness of these flames, and we constantly embrace their energies. In turn, we are blessed beyond measure by life.

Outside of Telos, in the area of the fifth dimensional Lemurian Crystal Cities of Light, we have temples consecrated to each one of the main sacred flames. These temples are quite large as a rule. The beings living in these areas tend and nurture the flames with their love, devotion and invocations around the clock. The fifth dimensional population is quite large, and the masters and angels of the sacred fires, as well as the priesthood of these temples, take turns tending and invoking the qualities and attributes of these flames. They do so in their own lives, as well as for the planet and for humanity. Their attention supports the energy required to maintain the level of perfection of the dimension they live in.

This type of ritual, dear ones, is done in every dimension. Angels of the sacred fires and angels from various choirs join in to support the many sacred flames we nurture. This is what makes the higher dimensions so beautiful and wondrous to live in. This activity went on in all temples in the time of Lemuria, Atlantis, Egypt and in all civilizations of previous golden ages.

It will soon become important for you on the surface to involve yourselves in the nurturing and expansion of these flames, for yourselves and for the planet. We have done this for ourselves and on your behalf for a very long time. Soon it will be required that all those living on the surface aspiring to ascend into a fifth dimensional state of being step into a more evolved level of spiritual maturity. You will be required by Divine Law to bring your own personal contribution to these flames, for yourself, humanity and the planet. It is a requirement in the fifth dimension for all those abiding there. Are you ready for a meditation now?

Meditation

Journey to the Violet Flame Temple in Telos

I ask now that you center in your heart and state your intention and desire to be filled with the wondrous energies of your divine presence. You may do this in this manner:

"In the name of the I AM that I AM, from the Lord God of my being, I ask now that every cell, every atom and every electron of my four-body system, all my subtle bodies, every particle of life that I am in all dimensions and states of consciousness, be filled with the wonders and the miracle energies of the Violet Flame of Freedom's Love. I now ask to be filled again and again, 24 hours a day, each day of my life." (Keep breathing it in.)

As you are being filled with the Violet Flame energies, set your intention to come with us on a journey with your higher self to the beautiful and wondrous Violet Flame Temple in the fifth dimension inside Telos. This temple has an etheric, fifth dimensional physical structure, and our people have access to it at any time, as you can, in your light body. In this temple, the Violet Flame burns perpetually, nurtured by the consistent love and devotion of our people, blessing all of life, mankind and the planet. This is a place where the Master Saint Germain spends much time with his twin flame Portia and with legions of Violet Flame angels of all the different choirs, recharging and attending the energies of this wondrous flame of God for the planet.

Keep breathing in the energy as much as you can, so you can bring this energy back to your physical body when you return to full consciousness.

Now see yourself standing in a large circular room with a high ceiling, where the Violet Flame is present everywhere. The walls are made of pure violet amethyst and the floor is made of amethyst crystal of a smoother texture and lighter color. Piercing through the amethyst wall you see many violet tone lights that give you the feeling of a mystical starry vision. The room is quite bright and you see dozens of fountains of all sizes and shapes emitting all possible shades of a violet hue, in a magical play of color and tone. Water fairies are having great fun playing with these energies. See them exulting in their playful joy. Flower fairies are also playing games creating beautiful flowers of all shades of white, gold and violet with this light energy. See them throwing some at you as their way of blessing and welcoming you. Open yourself to their joy and bliss. See also a great number of Violet Flame angels tending the Violet Fire with their love and adoration.

This great fire of the Love flame is not hot; it's on the cool side. There are several chairs in the room, and we ask each of you to choose the one you are drawn to in the area that feels the most comfortable to you. The chairs are made of pure violet crystal, and under each one is a flame of violet rising up to meet and enfold you. As it is burning up from underneath, it is entering and infusing every part of your body through the lower chakras. There is also another flame coming down from above, penetrating your crown chakra and infusing every cell of your body through all of the higher chakras.

As you consciously breathe it into your heart, you are being filled with the Violet Flame of Freedom like never before. There are several Violet Flame angels surrounding each one of you, pouring cups of love and cups of Violet fire into your energy fields and the various aspects of your life needing healing. The experience is different for each one of you. Keep breathing in the energy. Now see the Master Saint Germain with his Lady Portia and the Lady Quan Yin, the Goddess of Mercy and of Compassion, filling you with their love and imprinting your auric field with the flame of compassion, also a Seventh Ray energy.

We now ask you to open yourself to a greater level of compassion for your own healing and for the healing of those you love. Whatever it is you feel needs healing in your life, invoke the energies of compassion and forgiveness and allow the changes you want to take place. Stay in this state of bliss as long as you want. Talk to us, talk to Saint Germain or Quan Yin, the Goddess of compassion, and set your intention to completely heal yourself, including all the trauma of the past and the present. This room is filled with wondrous healing energy. As you sit and bathe in it, feel the waves of dark energy around and within your field wherever there have been problems, trauma or pain begin to lift and dissolve.

Feel a lessening of density. Feel how much lighter you are becoming. Feel the lightness and the sensation of joy infusing your being. As you feel greater joy, you lessen your burdens. Allow this lightness, this beauty, the love and power to nurture you in all ways. Keep breathing it in. Consciously request of the Violet Flame what you would like it to do for you. Sometimes, between your asking and the fulfillment of your request, clearing processes need to take place, but step-by-step you are working toward your victory. Do not feel rushed; take all the time you need.

When you feel ready, you can look around. Notice the guides, masters and angels willing to assist you if you have a query. The angels, by the way, especially those who work with mankind, come here to recharge with the Violet Flame vibration several times a week, or even on a daily basis. The unbalanced energy on the planet contaminates their forcefield, and they come here to cleanse and revitalize. We invite you to do the same. Stay with us as long as you wish. When you are ready, come back to full consciousness. Now, be mindful to not re-create through your thoughts, feelings and words the energies you have just transmuted.

We invite you to come back to this fifth dimensional temple any time you want. The door is now open to you. Master Saint Germain will always be there, and his angels are always ready to receive and love you, to assist you in any way that is needed. It is their great pleasure to lend their assistance.

As we conclude our talk this day in Telos, we honor all of you for your openness, sending our blessings of love, courage and wisdom. We also join our dear friend Saint Germain in sending waves of Violet Flame into the hearts of all those reading this material. And so be it.

Chapter Eight

Transition of the Soul, called Death, and Losing a Loved One in the Times to Come

Aurelia

Because there will soon be so many changes on this planet, and so many souls have made a conscious choice to depart their physical incarnation at this time, I know that many of us will be facing the physical transition of one or more loved ones. They have made, at this time in their evolution, a different choice than we have, therefore we need to start seeing the soul transition we call "death" from a different perspective. Ultimately, we all meet each loved one again, as our soul is immortal.

We all know there is no such thing as "death." Of course, there is a transition of the soul from a human experience in a physical body to another state, perceived as death, but for the soul this is simply a transition. For the soul, it always is a time of joy, release, freedom and reunion with other aspects of self. It is a time of liberation, reflection and new beginnings, never a catastrophic event. Once we fully understand this, we allow ourselves a grieving period, for this is how we honor the energy of those who have departed, but we never again feel sorry for the one who has left. We will be fully comfortable with the choice made by our loved one and in total allowance of it. We will thank them for the time and the love we shared together in this incarnation. We will bless them on their way to their new experience, knowing full well in our heart that separation is only an illusion of the third dimensional mind. We will know, without a doubt, that we can see and be with them again at any time on the inner planes, and that our connection with the ones we love can never be broken throughout eternity.

Those who love each other very deeply in an incarnated experience are usually those who have known each other, loved each other and incarnated within each other's life experiences for eons of time. We have experienced the physical loss of each other again and again, and we have also found each other and lived as friends or family time and time again.

Sometimes the transition, or death, occurs seemingly by accident or because of a crime, a war or a natural event that we call a tragedy. All transitions, no matter what form they take, are planned by the soul in another dimension. These choices are made for various reasons, according to the soul path or the balancing of karma that the one departing has willingly chosen. At the soul level, for the one leaving, this is generally a time of great excitement. He or she cannot wait to be on their way to their new experience and adventure in the great journey called "life."

Here is the story of a woman I know who lost her only son in a car accident. She felt totally devastated and could not bring herself back into a normal state of emotional balance. Finally, she asked me to channel Adama to find out why such a tragedy had come to pass in her life. She saw this event as a great injustice, and wanted to prosecute the one whom she felt was responsible for the death of her only son.

Here is what Adama replied to her through me. His words brought great relief and healing to her heart. Upon reading Adama's reply, she was able to release most of the pain and grief rather quickly. She was able to look at life again with renewed joy and hope, knowing that her son was alive and well on the other side of the veil, loving her more than ever, and doing exactly what his soul wanted to do next.

I feel it is important for all of us to understand more deeply this process of transition we call "death." We know that many of us, sooner or later, will encounter a similar situation either in our own lives or in the life of someone close to us. Those embracing this understanding in their heart and soul will be able to comfort themselves when confronted with such a situation. They will also be able to comfort others around them who have not yet embraced the grace of such an enlightened understanding of physical transition.

Adama Replies from His Home in Telos

Dear Lemurian Sister,

This is your brother and friend Adama. It is my pleasure to communicate with you this day, heart to heart. As I open my heart to you, I ask you to open your heart to me as well, to the truth of your being.

I feel your deep sorrow and pain regarding the loss of your beloved son. It is such a normal reaction for a mother's heart to grieve the loss of her child. Please dear one, it is important that you allow yourself to feel the pain and the grief, as it is not physically, nor spiritually, healthy to deny or repress one's pain. When you are ready, after a time, it is even more important that you release the pain and move on to your joy. Life must go on for all, as it never ends.

You have a beautiful open heart, dear sister, and the pain from the loss of your beloved son is a catalyst that is assisting your heart to reach greater opening. You know, dear one, there is no such thing as death. It is an illusion of third dimensional perception. If you could perceive beyond the veil, you would know that your son is alive, doing well and more aware than ever before. Your son now has the ability to understand his feeling toward you when in physical expression, and has been granted permission to come closer to you and to your heart than he ever did in his Earth life. He is now fully aware of the deep and true love you held for him, and his own heart is much more open. He also realizes that he did not return your love the way he could have, the way you hoped for. This is motivating him on this side of the veil to seriously review the lessons he wants to learn in his next incarnation.

You have had thousands of incarnations on this planet in the course of your evolution, and you have had thousands of children. You have incarnated with a great many of them again and again, and truly, you have never been separated very long from the ones with whom you had strong heart connections. Your son has been part of your life many times before, and he will be again, especially as the veils between the dimensions thin. In the years to come the veils will lift completely, and all of you will see your loved ones again face to face. In a not too distant future, as you commit to your ascension, you will experience the great joy of finding yourself again with all your loved ones who have departed the physical world. You will be with them again tangibly without having to leave your physical body. Can you imagine the spectacle and ecstasy this great reunion will create! It is part of the plan, my friend. Keep the candle of love and hope burning.

Feel the presence of your son around you, and feel the love that he is now returning to you. Since his transition, he has gained much new understanding that he was lacking while in his physical body. Your son petitioned the Karmic Board Council of Light for permission to be at your side very often, and to be allowed to become one of the guides assisting you in your next evolutionary step.

I, Adama, ask you to let go of the sense of tragedy. As far as your son is concerned, the accident he experienced was the working out of destiny, in spite of appearances. The man who hit him was the instrument of the settlement of a karmic agreement. Know that unless there was a soul choice by your son on the inner planes to end the present incarnation and move on to the next level, the accident would not have occurred. Ultimately, there was no accident, but the working out of soul choice for an evolutionary step.

At the level of the soul, it was not time for your son to come along in the ascension process as you have chosen for yourself. There were too many issues that needed to be worked out from a different perspective. Know that it would have been extremely difficult for him to work them out in the incarnated experience he just left. By choosing to leave his body at this time, your son now has an opportunity to prepare, with greater wisdom and understanding, his goals and destiny of his next incarnation. He will come back again in a few years as a wondrous child of the "new world" to grace the planet and assist others. In his next incarnation, he will be much better equipped emotionally to realize his dreams. He will be able to accomplish his goals with much greater ease than he would have been able to at this time.

Know that by making the choice to leave now, he will be able to ascend in the next life without all the pain, difficulty and hardships he would have encountered at this time had he stayed. Because of the great love you have had for him, you have assisted him in receiving this special dispensation for his next incarnation. He is most grateful for the love you have extended him so unconditionally while in the physical form.

Know that your son honors you for this love. He now lovingly assists you in preparing the way for your homecoming. Because you love your son so unconditionally, allow for the choice your son made to move on. From our perspective, and the perspective of his soul, leaving the incarnation was a timely and positive choice. Your son loves and honors you and truly desires to see you happy and in your joy. Your son does not want you to deny your grief, but he does want you to accept his departure as the best thing that could have happened to him at this time.

He is saying to you right now: "Mom, I am still alive and feel so much better. Life is so wondrous here, and I am preparing for our next reunion, which will be physical and tangible. It will not be so long until we meet again face to face, and you will know that I never left. During my seeming absence from your physical life, take this time to love yourself more, to become all the love that you are, and move into greater joy and aliveness." This is your assignment.

Your son wants you to contemplate more than ever your belief system around the life experience called "death." This event is also an opportunity to create within the Self a new leap in consciousness. Ask yourself, is there such a thing as death, or is it simply a transition from a physical experience to a greater reality? Do I really own my son, or does he belong to God, as do all other souls in evolution here and everywhere? Was my role as his mother primarily to sponsor and assist this soul in an incarnation on Earth, and through that, have we created bonds of love that will endure throughout eternity? Is my son really dead or is he alive and more vibrant than ever on another plane of consciousness? Is our separation a permanent one or just a temporary illusion? Can I choose to go on living in the love and embrace of my Divine Presence and really enjoy my life again without my son physically present, or will I choose to experience extended sorrow?

Dearest sister, I know your heart and I extend my deep love to you. Accept the gift of peace from me and move into your joy. Think about the death of your son's body as the caterpillar exploding into a brand new and happy butterfly. Become a butterfly yourself, and soon, the two of you will be playing, frolicking and laughing together in God's garden.

I am Adama, comforting your soul.

The wielding of great power is not necessary,
Nor is the understanding of great minds.
All that is required for ascension,
Individually or for the planet,
Is the awakening of your heart to the Truth.
- Adama

Part Two

Messages from

Various Beings of Telos

Let your heart listen
To the call of your soul,
And you will know
What the true purpose
Of your life experience is.
- Adama

Chapter Nine

Brotherhood of the Oak and Sisterhood of the Rose

Andal and Billicum

Greetings and blessings to our brothers and sisters of Mother Earth's interior and to those of you on her surface!

We are Andal of the Brotherhood of the Oak and Billicum of the Sisterhood of the Rose. We come to you today as emissaries of our people, for the purpose of expanding your awareness of another kingdom on the planet about which you know very little. Indeed, we are aware that you have yet many kingdoms to discover on your planet. As your consciousness expands to embrace the vibration of love in greater measure, the discovery of the other kingdoms will bring much joy and new songs to your hearts.

Together, as a very large family, we comprise a gathering of energies that represent both the plant and the crystal kingdoms *(including stones and minerals)*. We are a race of explorer beings, shall we say, who have investigated, stored and dispersed the full radiance of energies and beauty that are to be found in these kingdoms.

Our mission has been in process for millennia, and we have played an active role in the history of this planet since the time of Lemuria. Our existence predates Lemuria, but our awakening into service did not happen until the heart of Lemuria was awakened. We are beings who would appear smaller in stature than the images you have of our Lemurian cousins, but our energy signature is very long. If you were to view us in your realm, we, of the Brotherhood of the Oak, would look very much like your "hobbits" of popular literature. We, of the Sisterhood of the Rose, would look very much like your drawings of fairies.

In the etheric realm, however, the Brotherhood appears as very tall shimmering green beings who exude an extremely powerful energy that connects with you through your third *(or solar plexus)* chakra, and runs down through your lower chakras into the Earth herself. The Sisterhood appears like pulsing rose pink balls of energy that connect through your heart chakra and flow up to your seventh chakra to connect with Divine Source.

Together, we nurture the energies of human beings who inhabit the surface of the Earth whenever they journey into the natural realms in which we exist.

These journeys can be taken in the physical or the etheric realms. We are available whenever we are called to share with you, and we will imbue your physical and etheric bodies with the radiances of the plant and crystal kingdoms. To contact us and interact with us, simply set an intention to invite us into your energy. This will allow us to sample your current energetic state and provide you whatever is needed to balance your energy fields. We work closely with the consciousness of any crystals that may have within your environment, as well as the energies of the plants and trees that grow around you.

We have spent our incarnations on this planet exploring, cataloguing, understanding and creating various forms and methodologies to support the full radiance of each species of plant and crystal life. Each individual species, be it flora or fauna, rock or ether, has its own color, its own spectrum of radiance, and is aligned with its own ray vibration. Within this set of characteristics there are individual variations, as you move, for instance, through the considerable variety of roses. We have explored all of these and stored remembrances and qualities of all that we have experienced. In effect, we represent the living, breathing library of the plant and crystal kingdoms.

In this respect, we work closely with all the beings of Earth's interior to balance and harmonize the environments that have been created to sustain them. We also work with all beings on the surface that can and will harmonize with our energies. You know very well one such being, by the name of Edward Bach, from your recent Earth history. His work with flower essences was guided by his interactions with us in the etheric realms. His gardens and woods in the region of Great Britain were favorite places for our invocations for the radiance of the plant kingdom.

Many others have continued to increase his repertoire of essences, which are part of this re-emergence of plant energies and their usage to assist the surface population. Our knowledge of these energies is available to all who wish to experience and work with them. All you need to do is to contact us to receive our information. Indeed, these same energies may be drawn to you at any time, just by calling on the essence or energy by name. The same holds true for the energies and essences of the crystal and mineral kingdoms.

Our work with the guardians of the Inner Earth has been to safeguard these vibrations from the disruptions that have been part of the Earth's surface evolution. Each of us is a repository for a specific individual vibration. We hold this vibration from the time of birth, and pass it on to another at the time of our transition from this realm.

**We exist everywhere on the planet, and we
are part of a network of the Earth's
interior societies which have existed since
the inception of Earth's consciousness.**

We are in contact with all of these other societies, and we form a virtual university of information, experiences and vibrational impressions for all who wish to explore them.

We live for the most part in a dimension that is slightly beyond yours. As the third dimension transits into the fourth, we are just outside of your vision, so to speak, but can be seen easily by those who already see beyond the dimensional veil. Although we can lower our vibration and appear to you in your dimension with relative ease, we generally choose not to do so because we are part of the taskforce which is working to raise your vibration instead. If all of us in the fourth and fifth dimensions were to appear to you in your current state, there would be no motivation for you to move beyond it. We are in effect dangling a carrot to motivate you to take the steps necessary to raise your vibration and join us here in our dimension.

The Earth herself has taken that very same step of working very closely with us, as She is doing everything in her power to raise herself and humanity to the next level, and eventually to her fully ascended state. It is most important that we all work together toward the same goal to assist her in this awesome journey.

We invite you to call upon us whenever you wish.

You can call in the energies of any flower or tree and ask that the member of the Brotherhood who holds that signature appear to you. The same is true of the energy of any crystal. Simply call in the energy and ask that the member of the Sisterhood who holds that energy appear to you. This may happen on the etheric or the physical plane, depending on your openness to receive, but be assured that the contact will be there. The use of flower and crystal essences will also assist you in making this contact, for they provide a recognizable signature for the physical body to tune into.

We have begun to bestow on each child born on the surface today a set of characteristics that hold these vibrations within their DNA. Your "Crystal" children who are incarnating now hold these vibrations, and in fact, each child holds the vibration of a specific crystal. Subsequent generations will continue to be imbued with the various aspects of this energy until the full radiance of the crystal kingdom is present in the DNA of all people incarnated. Soon the surface populations will become a living crystal matrix of energy that holds the consciousness of the Earth in balance.

Generations of "Rose" children carrying within their DNA the pure essence of Earth's love are already incarnating on the surface. They are coming to heal the emotional body of Earth and to reinvest Her with the truth of her divine origins. Through this healing, the paradise on the surface you so long for will manifest. After a time, all who incarnate here will carry the full radiance of all of these vibrations, and our time in service on this planet will come to an end.

Those who reside within the Earth have long carried these energies within them. This allows for the creation and manifestation of crystal structures, of glorious, joyful and abundant ecosystems, and balanced energies within all their environments. This type of living will transform the surface worlds when these energies are fully embodied and understood, for the true nature of a crystal is to absorb and hold or act as a generator for the truest expression of Divine Source energy. The true nature of the heart is to create what one loves and love what one creates, without condition.

As your brothers and sisters who live within the Earth strive to help you open yourself more and more to the fullness of your vibration, we work together to provide magnificent tools for your awakening.

Our relationship with the current citizens of Telos is a collegial one. We are here to assist them in harmonizing the vibrations of the surface so that they may emerge in the near future to join the many incarnated Lemurians who live in the Mount Shasta area and across the planet.

We provide our assistance, in part, by adding specific energies to the grid that emanate from Telos through Mount Shasta. This grid is administered by Adama to assist in the re-opening of energies for all who live in the Mount Shasta area and in all areas on the planet where people are ready to embody their full Christed Presence.

This grid has many components and several levels of energy. Many different beings are employed in this work allowing Adama the fullest latitude in the transmissions directed through this grid. The grid itself is multi-dimensional, and indeed the citizens of Telos themselves are part of and transformed by its energies. We are all part of a much greater purpose. This grid comprises one of the many ways that energies are being harmonized on the planet at this time.

Adama, and his team in Telos, who seed the grid with the higher energetic life force necessary to penetrate the denser dimensionality of the surface, use our knowledge and library of vibrational signatures from various plants and crystals. We create an energy wave for each signature that is then sent through the grid so that its intensity may be harmonized to the first available level above the current surface vibration. At times, this wave is sent through at the second level of intensity above the surface vibration. Because these are times of more rapid transformation, two levels above is the highest we can generally transmit this wave so that the majority of surface beings can integrate it.

Our activities extend to all cities of the Agartha network, and also into the Middle and Inner Earth. In Telos, we have contributed greatly to the exquisite beauty that has been created there. This includes the materials used in their extended technology, their various modes of transportation and their food cultivation techniques which feed both the people and the animals. We also assist in creating the wondrous crystals that form the structure of most of their temples, as well as the beautiful stones used to construct their wonderful homes. We are able to work with them closely and assist in creating their miraculous lives because their vibration is one of constant love and harmony.

We share with you the love and support for your journey that your brothers and sisters in Telos do. There are many among us who wish to be among the first wave who journey out from the realms of Light within the Earth to meet with you personally. And this, my friends, we are hoping to do soon. The time has come for all who inhabit this beautiful planet to join together in love and brother/sisterhood as one family. We have already done so in the etheric, and it is time to do so in your realm. Your awareness, perceptivity and willingness is all that is needed to make this happen.

We live in a land of pure magic, the realm where unicorns and dragons roam the multi-hued forests and the songs of birds create pillows on which you can float. We live where you can converse with the clouds that carry your love back to the Source of All. In our dimension, all beings know and trust their intrinsic nature. The glow that is created from our love and harmony forms a blanket of energy that nurtures each one of us. We invite you to visit us whenever you wish and to cultivate the awareness of this realm in your everyday life. We invite you to plant in the garden of your heart, nurture the flowers of your dreams and uncover the crystals of your soul. We honor your tree of life in the forest of us all.

Many, many blessings, and great wishes of joy, for your safe return "Home" to the land of love and magic! We are Andal and Billicum, sharing with you the energies of the Brotherhood of the Oak and the Sisterhood of the Rose.

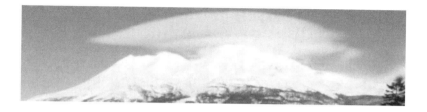

Chapter Ten

We are Crystal Beings

Billicum

The Sisterhood of the Rose exists, as do many other societies of crystal matrix energy workers, to hold the space for humankind and Earth herself to move into the fullness of their crystalline structures. The magnetic grid work that has been completed allows for the re-energizing of the crystal grid within the planet. This crystal grid is now growing in intensity again.

Structurally, crystals grow by adding on. The process involves the energies of transformation through the fire, earth and water elementals, which is, in truth, a blending together and a fusion of masculine and feminine energies. The pure crystalline form then becomes a transmitter of this combined energy. Within the structure of the human DNA, the same process is now beginning to unfold. You are adding on to your structure the formations needed to hold a higher and purer vibration.

Humans are beginning to open up fully and fuse within themselves the combined energies of the masculine and feminine. They are beginning to understand, on an energetic level, that the duality that exists within themselves, and within the planet herself, is actually a polarity that represents the

113

full spectrum of harmonics. They are now willing to embrace this polarity and enter into a new phase of development.

The evolution of Earth beyond the concept and experience of duality has begun.

Many of the recognized energetic spots on the planet, such as Sedona and most particularly Mount Shasta, have shifted their energetics away from a masculine or feminine vibration into a blended vibration that holds all the resonance of Divine spark and sacred feminine. Humankind itself has now begun that same journey. We of the Sisterhood of the Rose, like our counterparts in the Brotherhood of the Oak, are beings who serve the entire planet.

We have our planetary headquarters within Mount Shasta, and work very closely with all civilizations of the Earth's interior, including the Lemurian energies. It is the Lemurian energy, described as the Heart of Lemuria, that is leading the way forward in consciousness, in great service to this planet and surface humanity, in the preparation for the "great reunion." Along with all of the civilizations of the Inner and Middle Earth, we work together to create the energetic structures necessary to return the Earth to her own union with the Divine, and invest all who inhabit her with the community of heart that once existed here.

The children who are incarnating today already possess these new structures. They already have an innate understanding of the world beyond duality. They already connect to each other through an understanding of the strength of blended masculine and feminine aspects.

Those of you who are already here have the greatest, and in one sense most important, task.

You have held the resonance of the Earth, at her current vibrational level, in your systems the longest. It is with you that she most identifies herself as she evolves into a higher level of awareness. You all came here at this time for this significant purpose. As each of you adds on to your structure, she adds on to her own. As each of you opens your consciousness and heart to the fullness of the shift that is now taking place, she gains resources for her own evolution.

Your link in incarnation to those of us who hold these pure crystalline energies in the etheric is designed to express in the physical, these same energy structures. We are here to advise you in this, but we cannot predict for you or choose for you the path that this journey will take. It is up to each individual to chart the course that best suits his or her energies. We can and do hold the space for you to do this, assisting you with all of the options and potentials that exist.

You have the most important task, however, because it is in the physical that the greatest change must take place to assist the planet in her evolution and her awakening. You will feel much shifting in your physical bodies. Some may feel that organs are not functioning properly or that energy levels that have always been fairly stable now feel very different. You may feel a great and immediate need to change your diet in terms of what and how much you consume. You may feel a great desire to cleanse your bodies of emotional and physical toxicity that have built up over lifetimes upon lifetimes.

All these physical shifts must be honored, and the impulse to nurture your physical bodies must be heeded. Many products are and will emerge in the near future to nurture the body on a far deeper level than what is currently available in your commercial societies. It is important that you search for these products and share the information with your own communities.

You have always honored and incorporated the crystal communities into your lives. In modern times, we have inhabited your communication devices and computers, and we have held space for you through the jewelry and adornments that you wear. Many of you have also recognized us in our more natural forms and have carried us into your homes and temples.

Those of you who see us in the etheric have recognized our more human forms and greeted us as such. Understand that whatever way you choose to invite our energies in, we are here to support you in reaching the fullness of your potential in physical form. We are here with you to support the planet in reaching her highest potential in physical form.

The great central core of the planet, known as the inner central sun, is indeed a great crystal. It exists in a fifth dimensional vibration, broadcasting to the planet the vibration that she will be evolving to.

The great central crystal sun within the core of this planet is similar in its vibration and energetically supported by the great central crystal sun of this universe, which operates in a much higher dimension and energetic structure. The being known as the Great Crystal Master embodies this energy from the core of the great central sun of this universe, radiating and nourishing all other crystal suns. Using a vocabulary that you can understand, He is the supreme master, the head of all crystalline consciousness for this universe. In service to the Father/Mother God of this universe, Alpha and Omega, he allocates much of his energy and effort at this time in support of the great shift that is taking place, assisting in the resurrection and restoration of this planet to her original, glorious destiny. An important portion of His vast consciousness is here now, within the Earth, assisting and adding to your local inner crystalline central sun and all other crystals as well.

Around the planet, there are other fifth dimensional crystals that hold energies from the great central crystal. The crystals of the third and fourth dimensions that inhabit the planet get their form from this ring of fifth dimensional crystals. We, on the etheric side, are the consciousness in form of the great central crystal. We are one of the many representations of the love and light that shines from the heart of the planet.

Once the magnetic grid shift was completed, we were able to begin the next phase of our work on the planet. We have begun to work with groups of individuals, large and small, tutoring them in the workings of the crystalline grid, and the many healing and transformational techniques that are becoming available through this expansion. Each of these groups will soon begin to share the information on a global level that they have been given.

The function of the crystalline energies has always been two-fold. We are transmitters of energies beyond the physical world, and we are repositories of information. Today we begin that most important second part of our work, as the consciousness of humankind and the planet once again awaken to the information that we hold, and that we long to share with all of you.

You will hear us called by many names in the coming months. Many groups will contact us and manifest different parts of our mission on the physical plane. The work that each of you performs is part of this same great work. We will present ourselves to you in whatever form is most appropriate for the gathering or individuals involved, for each of you still carries a set of images and forms that we must connect with to reach you.

We ask you to first check in with your own knowingness and experience of us before accepting the images, forms or names that others have shared with you. Now is the time for all beings to trust their own knowingness, in whatever form it takes. The message from your heart is the most important aspect of this information, not the label or the image that presents itself to your conscious mind.

The ego of the human being is a powerful force, a necessary force, but one that must be integrated with the whole and not the only voice that is heard. The most important work in this regard, therefore, is to know yourself. It is through your own crystal center that we will communicate with you. Choose for yourself a physical crystal or crystals and work with them to experience the vibration of your own crystal center. Ask these crystals to attune themselves to your core vibration, and to then help you expand and evolve this vibration at a pace that is appropriate for you. As you complete your work with one set of crystals, be open to new crystal teachers who enter your path.

This is not a time for all to follow one model or mode of transformation. This is a time for each to follow his own model and to know that his or her work adds to the whole to create a new model or paradigm for the planet. The work that you do as individuals creates the group work, and the work that groups do together creates the society. As societies work together, the planet shifts.

I am Billicum from the crystal people, honored to be one of your teachers.

Chapter Eleven

Message from Posid

Galatril

Greetings my beloved brothers and sisters! I am Galatril, third-level member of the Council of Posid, beneath Mato Grosso in the country of Brazil. I have been in this position for many of your lifetimes and have spent much of my service reaching out to heal the energies of the past, and thus the present.

We who inhabit the resurrected city of Posid, now a wondrous and beautiful community of Light in the fifth dimension, and all of us living in other Atlantean energy cities within the Earth, recognize that there is great distrust for our vibration.

Many of you who experienced the cataclysms of the fall of Atlantis still carry the remembrance of emotional trauma and physical pain.

The energies of that experience, of the masculine overwhelming mental energies suppressing the feminine balance of the heart, still create emotions of fear and anguish within many of you, who might now be interested in initiating some kind of communication with us.

For this reason, we ask that you please allow yourself to

119

release these feelings about us that you hold through the mind and bring the energies of our deep love for you into your heart. Since the destruction of our continent, we have done much work to evolve our consciousness and embrace the energies of love from the heart. We have toiled steadfastly to rebalance the energies we so carelessly misused in the past. Today, it is with much joy and deep gratitude that we thank you for allowing us the opportunity to reach out to you and speak to your heart. If you will allow it, we can bring great healing to your soul and release of the trauma that so many, if not most of you on the surface, were subjected to in the past.

We who held ourselves in such high esteem in the Atlantis of old, and who rocked our planet so violently with our egos and misuse of technologies, have spent much time since in service to the Earth and the Earth's interior. We have lived in service to the elementals and nature spirits of this planet, and in service to our beloved Lemurian brothers and sisters, in order to balance the karma, the damage and the deep pain that was suffered by all of you. We have also learned much about the cravings of the soul for knowledge, and how these desires must be balanced by the deeper knowingness of the heart.

After the sinking of Atlantis, it was our Lemurian brothers and sisters who offered themselves and their expertise as mentors for our next evolutionary step. Many of our guides, our healers and teachers, who held the energies of compassion, wisdom and understanding to allow us to evolve, have been from Telos! Many were from other Lemurian cities as well. For a long time, their assistance, love and acceptance was for many, myself included, the only Light that shone in the very dark place within our hearts and souls. Our connection to them was the bond that has carried us higher and higher into the consciousness of love and true brotherhood, and we invite humanity to do the same.

We live beneath the region of Brazil because of the highly crystalline nature of the Earth in that area.

We are here now as guardians of these energies to keep them from being manipulated again by those who do not reflect or understand the Divine Plan. In the past, we would have insisted on utilizing the tremendous force of this energy for power, domination and control, but today we are its protectors. It is now very appropriate for us to be the guardians of these energies, because we have the fullest understanding of them through our experience of our misuse of them. We can follow their flow with great precision evolved through millennia of observation. We do this in service to our Lemurian brothers and sisters, whom we now consider our very dear "family." They are the synthesizers and harmonizers of these energies at this time of the planet's transformation.

In many ways, our lifestyles are very similar to those of Telos. All of us hold positions of responsibility within our community. We also spend much time in service to the planet and our brothers and sisters now incarnated on the surface. A great deal of our work consists of programming crystal tools that are emerging on the surface at the present time. We have the technology to create, from the organic structure of the subterranean levels of the Earth, a new form of crystal that emits a much higher vibration of energy than what has been previously available on the surface.

These crystals are now beginning to surface, and will interact with the environments into which they are introduced to provide a detoxifying effect on all levels of denser vibration. They are very open to the conscious intention of the individuals who wish to work with them, and will work with all who ask to. They will, however, express only one intention at a time, and only if the vibration resonates with the Divine Plan. This is the first layer of healing tools that will begin to emerge. These crystals also reflect the color vibration of the individual who is currently working with them, and may change color if or when transferred to a different person.

Our buildings in Posid are made of a very similar crystal material. This energy has greatly contributed to the healing of our toxic emotions, as well as the toxic emotions of the Earth herself. We hold in our hearts a great desire to be of assistance to the surface populations at the appropriate time. We wish to contribute and support you in the creation of your own cities of Light with these same healing materials. In addition, these crystals will be available to heal your soil, to re-energize your food and water supplies and more.

> *We want to assure you that all of us hold a very great desire in our hearts to manifest, in all our actions and interactions with you, the love and compassion needed to recreate a united civilization on this planet.*

It is our heartfelt goal to assist in the manifestation of this unity consciousness for the planet, in all of Her dimensions and realms. We wish to experience with you again, face to face, the love that will bring the highest joy and grace to all living on the surface.

It has become appropriate for us now to say that in the higher realm of the fifth dimension, Atlantis and Lemuria are fully manifesting the energies of the original plan for these continents. Atlantis, representing the energies of the Divine Father, and Lemuria, representing the energies of the Divine Mother, were meant to work together in the consciousness of divine union. We were to assist, in love and unity of consciousness, not only the people of our respective continents, but also to become loving guides and mentors, role models of unity, for other civilizations evolving on the planet as well.

In recognition of the great number of lifetimes that many of you have spent attempting to distance yourselves from the vibrations of Atlantis, we ask you to work with us on a simple meditative exercise. We hope this meditation will assist you in cleansing the traumatic vibrations of old so that the new vibration of love and harmony may seed itself in the evolving consciousness of the planet.

There were skills and technological resources created in Atlantis that many of you have direct knowledge of. It is time for these technologies to resurface, albeit in a vibration of love and service, not ego and power. As you clear these old energies and experiences, all that was good, all the wonders of Atlantis, will rise to the surface through you.

Neither the continent of Atlantis nor the continent of Lemuria are destined to rise again in the physical.

They will be reborn instead through the energies of those incarnated at this time. The gifts and resources of these civilizations will be re-created and re-manifested, in new and shining forms by those of you living on the surface today.

We invite you to journey with us now into the crystal heart of your soul. Envision a glowing center that resides behind your heart and transmits energy in undulating, pulsating waves throughout your body and into the energy field of the Earth herself. Your crystal center vibrates in resonance with the crystal center of the Earth. As you focus on your own crystal central sun, reach out with your knowingness, with your love, to the crystal central sun that sits in the core of the Earth.

Follow the trail of energy as it leaves you and travels into the Earth and watch for the images that appear along these waves of energy. These images may appear to you as colors or sounds. They may be scenes from the time of Atlantis. They may be geometric shapes or the images of people you have known. In each instance, reach out to these images, bathing them and surrounding them in the pulsating waves of love that are emanating from your crystal heart, your sacred heart.

Do not try to explain or interpret these images. That knowledge will come in a time of its own choosing, when appropriate. Simply envelope these images, these energy transmissions from the time of Atlantis, in the overwhelming love that you now offer in service to the planet and humankind. Bring each of these remnants of energy, these orphan energies, into the oneness that exists between your central sun and the central sun of the Earth.

Allow the pure energy of the Divine to heal and re-inform these energies.

Allow and surrender to the Divine plan that holds all of us in its loving hands. And most of all, allow yourself to release eons of pain and sadness, of guilt and shame. You who are incarnated now are not responsible for the errors in judgment made during the time of Atlantis.

You are not responsible for righting any wrongs, for in truth, there were no wrongs. There were merely the lessons learned by a civilization that had chosen a particular path of understanding. That path involved one of the greatest collective initiations ever experienced on this planet. We who lived in the time of Atlantis, and many of you were with us, chose to experience, from every angle, the separation between mind and heart. We created experiences by choice to highlight that learning.

Today we reach out again, in greater knowingness, to communicate to you all that we now understand. We ask those of you who were here with us to reach out with your awareness of these times, and communicate the same to those living around you. We do not wish to recreate the Atlantean cities of old. We wish to create with you new communities that grow and evolve from the love that we share.

We will never again introduce technologies that will create a separation of mind and heart.

We will bring our technologies into your consciousness only when you have reached an anchored vibration of love, harmlessness and community. You will then create these tools in the fourth or fifth dimensional plane of existence. You will add to them new and wonderful tools and technologies of your own.

We have gathered much wisdom from our civilization that perished due to our lack of inner vision. We long to share what we learned with those who administer your surface governments at this time. With open hearts, we invite all you who so desire, and those who have connections with us from incarnated experiences on our former continent, to visit us here in Posid. Journey here in your etheric bodies, and study with us the consciousness that led to the fall and eventual destruction of Atlantis. We now open our doors and have created special quarters in our city to receive all who wish to reconnect and interact with us. We invite you to come and observe, with love and without attachment, the weaknesses and imbalances that were created then. We wish you to carry these lessons back to the surface, so this wisdom can imprint the consciousness of those who now govern your dimension, some of whom harbor the same destructive impulses and could create the same mistakes again.

While the halls of visitors and nightly classrooms of Telos are overflowing with ever-increasing numbers who are enjoying new training and reconnection with many former friends and family members, ours are almost empty.

With great anticipation and love, we invite you to come here in your dream states, and visit us in our Atlantean home.

There is so much our hearts long to share with you. We promise to give you just as pleasant and heartfelt a reception in Posid as you are receiving from your Lemurian brothers and sisters in Telos. As much as you long to reconnect with your Lemurian family, we long to reconnect, heart to heart, with all of you as well. Nearly all of you have had incarnations in Atlantis and we consider you our former family members as well.

The beauty that Posid once displayed in the physical has been replicated in the fifth dimension, though with much greater grace and perfection. You will be just as delighted to visit Posid as you are to visit Telos and other Lemurian cities. We live a life of magic and paradise that we wish to share with you as a sample of your future.

The doors of Posid are open for all who wish to rekindle friendships of the past.

Eventually, we will play our role in association with the Lemurian emergence to the surface, and we will once again walk among you. We thank you for your understanding and for this opportunity to be heard through this publication. We bless you for your hearts that love us still.

I am Galatril, Atlantean brother of the past. On behalf of my brothers and sisters in Posid, we send you our love and compassion, and our deepest friendship and support.

Chapter Twelve

The Children of Telos

Celestia, Elder of Telos

Greetings from Telos, I am Celestia. Today, we have a class of younger and older children who would like to answer many of the questions you have. Needless to say, they are very excited about this opportunity. Our children spend much time studying the surface situation, as they are eager to understand and communicate with your children.

The first thing the children would like me to communicate to you, and most particularly to the children of the surface, is that they are in many ways envious of the experiences that take place there, even though envy is not truly an emotion we focus on here in Telos. The children of the surface have been given a most exciting adventure during their incarnation. They have chosen to incarnate at a time when there are extraordinary changes taking place on Earth, a time when everyone's energies are so important to these changes.

We are all living in a time when transformation is not just a wish or a goal, but rather a growing reality. Each individual living on the surface during this time, who is incarnated in a third, and soon to become a fourth and fifth dimensional physical body, is an explorer, discovering new worlds and new ways of being.

You, the children of Earth, have gathered together for this life, in many languages and locales, to create a group project, shall we say, or a group mural of energies that are pure and distinct from the current energies of the surface. You have gathered together to share in a great celebration of creativity, and each of you has brought new and wonderful gifts to this gathering. Each of you carries a precious piece of the vision that this planet will soon experience. You have come here to create the bridge between the old and the new world.

In truth, the change has already taken place
on many levels and in many dimensions.

Now, it is for everyone on the surface to begin experiencing the awareness of the changes and the choices that all have made to bring these new energies into reality. Each of you incarnated at this time possesses the knowingness of this new reality. It is not with the spirit of sacrifice that you have incarnated on the surface at this time and in this space. Your heart is grateful and joyous about the transformation you are beginning to experience.

Many of you have trained for this adventure here in the schools and classes of Telos. With us, you have studied the cultures and energy patterns of the surface world. You have communicated with beings on the surface who have been living there for many years, as advance scouts shall we say, preparing and holding the space for this grand adventure. You have sampled and canvassed the soul imprints of many family groups before deciding what family you would incarnate into. Many of you incarnated on the surface communicate regularly with your study groups here in Telos, for it is indeed an ongoing group effort between the surface and the Inner Earth communities.

You regularly send back reports of your activities on the surface, and most importantly your reactions and emotions within the intensity of a third dimensional incarnation. You send us mental accountings and visual images, as well as the understandings that you gain from working within the denser energies of the surface. This information is of great importance to the children here in Telos. They are interested to know, not only how your adventure is progressing, but also how they can best assist you to bring about the transformations that you intend to accomplish on the surface.

Message from Luriel

Luriel is one of the elder boys in the class.

Warm greetings from your brothers and sisters, from your playmates and classmates in Telos! We are almost beside ourselves with the excitement and joy of communicating with you directly. Though we may appear to be separated from you, we are actually right beside you during much of your adventure on the surface. We follow most avidly the work being done with the Psychic Children, as they have been termed by your elders. These are our friends who bring much awareness to people of all ages. These children are, in fact, very old souls who are delighted with this opportunity to share their knowingness and awareness with the planet. They do so in the "guise" of a child, without the responsibilities and burdens that seem to plague so many of the adults on the surface.

They are able to carry out their mission as play, and this is a most wonderful example for all on the surface. They are doing their best to live out the truth that we live here in Telos, that all work is play and that all knowingness comes from the innocence of experience. Joy is truly an experience of innocence, and your psychic children are here to model this for you.

All children incarnating now on the surface carry an

enhanced vibration. Their DNA has been upgraded, shall we say, to allow for higher levels of communication and awareness. They have not entered this incarnation separated from their understanding of who they are and why they are on the surface at this time.

They have been given many names, such as Indigo, Psychic, Crystal, Violet and others. In truth, these names refer to the class they are entering with.

Just as on the surface, you all enter into school as part of a future graduating class, such as the class of 2012, each of these children is part of a class joined prior to incarnation. Each class was given a different assignment on the surface, and each assignment carries a different vibration. All classes, assignments and vibrations are part of the same school, just as we, in Telos, are part of this same school.

All classes are connected via a grid. This is the grid you have heard so much about from the Psychic children who use it to communicate with each other. But the entire grid is much greater than all of its individual parts, and forms a communication system for the entire universe. This grid is a creation of the energies of the Divine Plan. It is entered into through the energies of the heart. It connects all beings in the Universe, much as your Internet does on the surface. The Internet is, in fact, a third dimensional representation of this grid, although its true function and usage has yet to be discovered and utilized. Your Internet will eventually transform as the consciousness on the surface transforms.

Some of the psychic children spent time in Telos or other Lemurian-energy cities prior to their incarnation. Some come from other soul and planetary groups. But they are all here to foster fun, community and joy. Approximately a third of the children who live in the area of Mount Shasta have been sent from our own ranks here in Telos. We have sent many children as well to other cities and families around the planet. We could, in effect, call this a student exchange or study travel experience, as you do in some of your schools. Here we view it as an incredible opportunity to practice all that we have been taught, and to experience an extraordinary adventure that far exceeds anything we could imagine.

Many of us have been called to the Emissary ranks in our school here in Telos. I am one of these. We are ambassadors of fifth dimensional energies who travel to generate and hold this loving vibration, in order for the citizens of the surface to experience and acclimate themselves to this vibration. We do so on assignments that range from days to years *(in your surface timeframe)*. We also do so in groups or individually, but we always report back all information, observations, experiences and understanding to the entire class. The class itself then presents all that they receive to the citizens of Telos and the High Council. We too are a part of the ongoing work of Telos.

Students on the surface are set apart from society as a rule. You study for many years and then you make a leap into society upon graduation. Students in Telos are always included in society, and contribute a particular and special energy in the discussions and decisions that govern our world.

Some of the younger children wish me to send their love and an image that they all carry with them in a special place in their hearts. This vision is of a great cavern that sits inside the mountain. It is so enormous by surface standards that you cannot see the sides or the top of it, so you might think you are out on the surface rather than inside the mountain. There are many special places to visit in this cavern. The one the children wish to take you to now is on the shore of a great lake. All around are hills and dales from which water falls in glorious colors and then travels to the lake. The rainbows formed by these falls continue into the waters of the lake and create small glowing waves of color that wash onto and decorate the multicolored sand on which the class sits.

All of the children of the class are present for a picnic, and they invite you to join them. The picnic is for study and play because they want you to see how it is all the same. The younger students are themselves teaching the lessons today. The teachers and elders are all sitting among the students to enjoy the class. Each lesson is taught in the form of a story or a song that each student has created.

They invite you to listen to these stories and songs, and then create one of your own to share with the class. They ask that the lesson you create be one about the surface, from your present incarnation. Although they monitor all that happens above ground, your impressions are unique. They wish to learn, to grow and to experience directly the wonders of the adventure that you are presently having on the surface.

You may visit us at our picnic whenever you wish, for all will gather when we hear your call. In the multi-dimensionality in which we exist here in Telos, we can gather in many places and in many aspects at once, to enjoy your stories and songs, even if we are engaged in other activities. We bless you and look forward to playing with you in Telos whenever you wish to visit. Soon, we will all play together on the surface, when the consciousness increases enough to allow us to come out. For now, we invite you to engage in play with the children around you, for we are they. Warm blessings.

Message from Angelina

One of our teachers, Angelina, a healing master and elder in Telos, would like to address a question asked regarding the hyperactivity of children on the surface.

I am Angelina, and I wish today to speak to both the children and the adults on the surface regarding hyperactivity and the use of certain drugs to "control" it. Hyperactivity is not understood by your so-called "authorities" on the surface. Much of the hyperactivity demonstrated in this present-day generation of children is in fact their reaction to the overwhelmingly unhealthy environment in which they live. Because of the artificial way of life you have created life on this planet, your precious children are forced to experience constant and abnormal over-stimulation of the pituitary and pineal glands, as well as their physical senses.

Much has been said about diet and exposure to your media of television, music and movies. These are also serious concerns.

The constant bombardment of the senses by the microwave technologies and wave forms that enter your energetic and physical bodies from television sets, cell phones and microwave ovens disrupts the important ongoing transformation of DNA structure that all these children have come to manifest. In your major cities, the disruption is so great that it is a wonder children and adults can function at all. Each day brings a new invasion of your energy structure by man-made energies that do not work well with the Divine Flow.

These energies seek instead, by their nature, to invade and overwhelm the very energetic foundation around you. This technology is not dark per se, but the use and/or misuse of it has created much of the darkness and distorted energy patterns that currently affect you and your children. It interferes dramatically with your intrinsic energetic patterns.

It is very important that you assume responsibility for providing as clean an environment as possible for your children to live in, and especially to sleep in. Bedrooms filled with televisions, VCRs, CD systems, cell or electronic phones, electronic clocks, and other such items *must be avoided.*

Children must be given a clean environment in which to regenerate and restore balance each evening. The level of toxicity in your foods, your building materials and your environment must be addressed and corrected. This situation is not conducive to their maturation and evolution in the manner needed for them to accomplish the goals they came here to manifest.

The build-up of heavy metals in your children's physical systems is a major contributor to hyperactivity, as well as other nervous and systemic conditions.

Water, clean water, is a daily necessity for these children, as well as for everyone else. In general, the liquids you and your precious children ingest through your mouth daily are harmful to your body and soul. You must work to clean up your water supplies and remove the toxic chemicals, such as fluoride. Those of you who live in cities must filter your water before drinking, and use natural products for bathing that are free of toxic chemicals.

There are many effective natural products currently available to you that will reduce levels of toxicity, rather than the culturally fashionable ones. Use them daily to ensure that every member of your family has a vital life force and a balanced system. You must reduce or eliminate the amount of soda pop, artificial drinks, coffee, alcoholic beverages and other toxic substances that you have become so accustomed to ingesting as part of your daily diet. Pure water still remains the main source of liquid that will assist in re-balancing the body to its natural and healthy state.

The solution for children is not to medicate them, but to correct the imbalances created in their bodies by their environment. What is needed to achieve this balance is different for each child. In any healing crisis, each individual has a set of characteristics that requires a unique healing tools. The process of healing should be entered into, in a supportive way by both parents and children together. In many cases, the child may not recognize the hyperactivity, but knows only that he or she is not functioning in a way adults and society expect. Such a situation creates guilt and shame for the child, and it is imperative that this kind of circumstance be avoided.

> *We are beings who desire balance, and the more a child can be shown how to achieve that balance, the more he will gravitate toward it.*

The new children are here to guide us to a greater understanding of what will maintain and balance the energies of the surface at this time. They are here to lead us to a more gentle manner of living and a more heart-centered approach to all relationships, both personal and social.

My first suggestion is to take your children to a healer, or as you call them on the surface, a medical intuitive, who has had experience with children. Ask for a snapshot of your child's current energetic state, for it is important to remember that the physical symptoms of hyperactivity are simply the body's reaction to an energetic imbalance. There are many natural methods that can be used to balance your child's energy bodies. These include herbs, flower essences, exercise, meditation, yoga, chi gong and tai chi. Children will benefit greatly from a mineral rich and balanced diet of good fruits, vegetable, grains and an adequate amount of healthy protein, because growing children in your environment still need sufficient quality protein. Their diet should be a balance of all factors, as should yours, including acid/alkaline mix, natural rather than processed sugar content, vegetable versus animal protein, and sufficient living foods versus dead processed foods.

There is also a great deal that can be done energetically through chakra balancing and color and crystal therapies. Toning and drumming are very supportive to the system.

Music therapy is a soothing form of balancing for hyperactive children. Session work, in groups or individually, that involves both verbal and energetic therapy also supports their re-balancing. Creative therapies such as painting, drawing and writing are also very beneficial. Video games and excessive television are not the answer.

Children who have incarnated on the surface now are working to re-balance their brain chemistries, their endocrine systems and their physical senses in order to access and run a higher vibration of energy. They have entered into incarnation with a different limbic system than you possess and a clearer perception of what their life force should feel like.

They will rebel against all attempts to force them into a way of being that does not intrinsically resonate with their true divine nature.

They will "short-circuit" at a greater rate than any prior generation if not given a suitable nurturing, calming and supportive environment in which to live. Their need for a true heart-supported community is very strong. The ties they bring with them from communities such as Telos and others will vibrate strongly in their emotional bodies. They must be nurtured properly. They will gain much from group situations where they are invited to participate in community, civic and school activities that allow them to be creative and responsible and interact with people of all ages.

Allowing older children to work with younger children as mentors, and adults with children as guides and muses creates wondrous connections that will open hearts and assist the transformation of the core of your society.

In truth, the things that will help your hyperactive children are available all around you, without the assistance of pharmaceutical drugs. You need only make positive changes in your environment and also the children's. There is no need to drug their systems to control, in a very synthetic manner, behaviors that your society deems inappropriate. It is counter-productive to recognize the symptom but refuse to admit and address the underlying cause. The solution comes from the use of tools and skills that you already have around you to assist your children.

These children are here to give you the opportunity to manifest mutual help and cooperation.

In Telos, we are here to support you and your children. We are here to show you how you can bring balance into your lives and theirs.

The teachers, healers and children of Telos reach out every day to the children of the surface. We send them our love, our blessings, and we look forward to the time when contact and communication become more direct. We invite the precious children of the surface to visit us in Telos in their dream state, as we share with them our heartfelt desire to play in a vibration of peace, compassion, love and light. Until we speak again, we wish them, and all of you, much joy and laughter.

Message from the Children of Telos
Through Celestia and Angelina

We are the children of Telos. We meet you in your dreams to let you to know that we love you. We like to sing to you of times to come when we will once again be united as one. The soul remembers and then sets out to create a new song for all of us to remember. We want you to know your song and the elements of who you are as we journey, across time and space, in all the colors of the rainbow to join you. As we guide you, we sit at your feet and we stroke your heads with love and comfort.

We send you our message of peace and understanding through every flower that greets you and every bird song along your path. We stand arm in arm with the divine host and broadcast a vibration of forgiveness and unconditional acceptance for all beings of the Earth. As your heart and your inner knowingness pick up the frequency of this broadcast, we ask that you listen and feel the pulse of our energies in your soul.

When we speak, we also speak with your voices, and when we sing, you hear words long forgotten that you once sang. You feel the melodies that we sang together long ago and you begin to create new melodies from the old. We all sing together in a harmony which has never before been experienced. As we create these new songs, the whales, the solar wind and legions of angels join us. We sing with voices that grow stronger with each passing day, and all beings rise up in celebration of this new vibration that encircles the planet. We celebrate the joy that we share with each one of you.

You wander through what appears to be bleak times, and yet, they are in fact the brightest. The family and friends from the Inner Earth and distant stars that you long to join are already with you. You just need to recognize their frequency around you.

Listen for the tones we send you. Hear them in your ears and realize that they are real and not a product of your imagination. We are contacting you in your soul. You may hear a ringing or a chime, or you may hear a harp or soft voices. You may hear a buzz or a simple tone. These sounds may last an instant or go on much longer. Know that it is the children reaching out to you, playing back for you the song we sing to train your ears and human minds to recognize and communicate anew with this vibration.

When you are in bed at night and the world of man-made objects around you is quiet, reach out with your hearing and your heart. Call to us with your intention and we will answer. Listen for the song that beckons us all home to a wonderful gathering of loved ones. Soon, the sound will become familiar and part of your waking hours. Sing to us as we sing to you. Our love for you knows no bounds and our hearts always play with yours. We love you.

In your evolution, most of you
Have ignored the promptings of the heart.
You have lost your ability
To recognize that the heart
Is the great intelligence of the soul.
- Celestia

Chapter Thirteen

Antharus, The Blue Dragon Speaks

Dialogue Between Antharus and Aurelia Louise

Greetings, my love, I am Antharus, the Blue Dragon. You and I have known each other for a very long time, and our friendship has endured the test of time.

I returned to Earth from the Pleiades about a year ago, to spend time at your side once again, even though you are not yet able to see me with your present vision. Yes, I left your planet over 100,000 years ago when dragons became feared and hunted. This was a time when a great number of people on the planet lost their connection with their divine source. That era became the second phase of what you call "the fall" in consciousness, when humanity entered further into density and duality.

I want you to know that you and I are good friends from a distant past on this planet, when dragons were honored, loved and appreciated as guardians and protectors of your civilization and the Earth. Because of the quality of friendship you and I shared for so long in Lemuria, I have returned to offer my deepest friendship to you. I bring my contribution to the transformation of your planet in ways you cannot yet understand. It is my intention to assist you to embrace more magic and fun in your life; soon, my

141

beloved, you will begin to understand what I am saying. Allow yourself to access the remembrance of the wondrous times we shared together and how much fun we used to create in the time of Lemuria.

I am a light being and have been living in fifth dimensional consciousness for a long time, and thus, not visible to those whose inner vision has yet to reopen. I have maintained my 30-foot stature, and when my wings are fully spread open, you would need a measuring tape about 75 feet long to reach from one tip to the other.

In the time of Lemuria, I was the leader of a group of dragons who faithfully and graciously guarded your palace and many wondrous temples.

We, as dragons, enjoyed our service to life for hundreds of thousands of years in the glorious time of Lemuria, when all of life was perfectly harmonious. In spite of our great size, people did not fear us, and children delighted to play with us. We often allowed them to sit in the safe place between our great wings and took them for flying rides over the land.

You too, Aurelia, like the children, would enjoy sitting in the safe dent in the bone structure between my wings, and together we would fly great distances at great speed, soaring through the sky of the Motherland. Today, within the consciousness of your present society, if I were third dimensional and physically solid, such fun would be considered quite dangerous and unthinkable. In our time, fear did not exist on the planet. When fear is absent, total safety exists. You often used my body and my flying abilities to transport yourself from one place to another. One could say in your present day language, that you used me as a private taxi service. This may seem odd to your current perception, but in those days there was no such limitation. It happened with my total willingness to take you wherever and whenever you wanted to travel in this manner. Think of it as a mutual cooperation, as two friends taking off together for shared fun and enjoyment.

Also understand that in those glorious days, before the fall in consciousness, the world was not dense as it is today. Almost everyone could raise and lower their vibration at will between the third and fifth dimensional frequencies, according to the particular activities they wished to play with.

When you came flying with me through the skies of the Motherland, both of us would raise our frequencies to the fifth level, thus becoming quite light in vibration. This is why there was no danger of falling, as we both had total control of our bodies. In view of the present density human bodies, flying through the skies on the wings of a dragon would be not only dangerous, but impossible. In our time, flying, teleporting and levitating were common knowledge which everyone took for granted. We never even considered life without these abilities. They were considered part of our divine nature and our birthright to enjoy for eternity.

When the dragons moved into other dimensions, humanity lost much of their ability to experience life with ease and grace. What was natural then would be considered magic today, and the grace with which people lived gradually dwindled to a mere memory. Your ancient memories are veiled under a thick curtain of fear and forgetfulness. Today you yearn to rediscover the way to manifest magic in your lives, as you did in ancient times. For those choosing to embrace full enlightenment and self-realization through ascension in this life, these gifts will be yours again to enjoy. The magic you once experienced will return in even greater measure, because you have been deprived of these abilities for so long. Dear one, humanity will never again take these gifts for granted and misuse them, as in the past. The understanding you have gained from the many lifetimes of experiencing disconnection from your Divine nature will keep you on the path from now on. The lifetimes of suffering and struggle reinforce this understanding in a way that mere teachings could not have. Experience is, after all, the best teacher.

I can read your thoughts, and your mind is racing a hundred miles wanting to know what you can do and where you can go for me to physically materialize in front of you. I feel your excitement. At least, you are not afraid. This pleases me. Well my beloved, the time is not appropriate yet, but hopefully will be in the near future. I will have the opportunity and permission to show myself to you tangibly, so that you can see me with your physical vision and know me once again.

I have made my abode at this time quite high on the south side of majestic Mount Shasta, in an area where it is quiet and I can live undisturbed. As I am not visible to anyone, all is very pleasant. Actually, where I live now is very close to the area I used to enjoy spending much of my free time in the time of Lemuria. The fourth dimensional aspect of the mountain is a place of exquisite beauty and comfort. Some day, when your inner sight opens more, you will see and enjoy it all. You will be living in two worlds, and eventually in three, and even much more.

Aurelia - How did it come about that dragons had to leave this planet? What really happened?

*Antharus - As dragons, we possess full mastery of the elemental realm. This means that we are equally at home in the air, on land, under water and engulfed in fire.

If you were to look back upon Earth history, you would see that almost every culture makes various references to dragons, at least in stories and mythology. I wish to remain humble here, but I must state the facts. The beauty, power and majesty of dragons were such that many humans, who had strayed from their connection with Love and divine source, became envious of our powers and decided to bring us under the dominance of their arrogant spirit. Many thought that they could possess, control and use us in any way they pleased.

Few beings on Earth at the time could match the intelligence, compassion, strength and beauty of dragons, perhaps only the beautiful and gentle Unicorn.

Dragons are great lovers of freedom, having attained even then a great level of spiritual mastery. There was no way we would allow ourselves to submit to being enslaved by the will of primitive humans. Yes, I say primitive, as this is what it was for us.

Because dragons were masters of the elements, it was believed that we possessed a certain kind of magic which could be transferred to others. Almost overnight, humans and dragons became adversaries, after hundreds of thousands of years of mutual love and cooperation. Of course, it was not all humans, and you, my beloved, sought with all your might to protect dragons. You were one of those who secretly provided food, shelter and sanctuary to many of us. *(Dragons were vegetarian, contrary to popular mythological belief.)* In exchange for sanctuary, the dragons offered protection and kinship to their benefactors and companions. Because of your influential position at the time, you did all you could to stop the massacre and enslavement of dragons, but you were not able to erase the ignorance of the people or interfere with their free will. I remember how much grief this caused you at the time and for long after.

At some point, humans decided that the dragons' magic must emanate from our blood, as we had such great strength and longevity. Then, the hunt for our blood began. Adversaries now became real enemies as the human race endeavored to slay every dragon they could find. Many dragons perished, while others sought sanctuary where they could, mostly in very remote regions of the world. This attempt to hide from our slayers contributed to our image as solitary creatures, rather than the social beings we once were. The extreme temperatures of our new homes changed the color of our skin and its appearance. Eventually, the dragons that survived were invited by the galactic spiritual hierarchy of the time to be transported to the Pleiades. This is when I chose to leave the Earth in search of a friendlier home. Many other dragons chose to go to the Pleiades, while others went to other host planets.

Originally, dragons were a greenish-gray color, with a skin texture similar to that of an elephant. Our ability to control the elements allowed us to evolve to the scalier, reptilian skin you have seen in illustrations. The color of our skin became associated with the geographical area of our new homes, and it was not uncommon to hear that a blue, green or even a red dragon had been sighted. These were the saddest times of our existence.

The dragons kept their distance from the human population, as they could no longer trust them. Their vast numbers dwindled to a precious few. Whenever there is a great loss like this in any world, it is felt throughout all the kingdoms. This loss was no exception. Humans realized the error of their ways far too late.

There are many places where the Earth's ley lines intersect. Some of these places allow one world to connect with another. You may have heard certain expressions that refer to the "lifting of veils or mists." In certain places and at certain times, it is possible to do just that, to literally cross over into another or parallel world. Most of the dragons who did not leave the Earth made their way to these doorways and are now living at peace on Earth, but in another plane or dimension, unseen by the third dimension.

There are still a few dragons in your world.

They live in remote caves, caverns and pits. Those who have

chosen to remain patiently wait for humanity to awaken to the truth that all beings and all species are part of a great brotherhood, and that one species is not less or more than another. In the meantime, their energy is very healing to the planet because it is elementally so balanced. Fortunately for them, any sightings are met with disbelief.

At this time, many dragons have returned to assist the planet and humanity to regain a balance with the elements. Without this support, the Earth and humanity could not make the necessary shift into the higher dimensions without great disturbances to the elemental planetary forces. Of course, many of us are here in the physical, but invisible to your sight, as we vibrate to the frequency of the Light Realms of the fifth dimension. This way, we can do our work in peace, undisturbed by humans. We know that more than 99% of the people on the planet would experience great fear if we were suddenly seen, especially in large numbers, and once again we would be hunted.

We also know that there will come a time, not so far away, when humans will reconnect with the various aspects of their divine nature. They will once again perceive all sentient beings as equal aspects of Creation, and we will once more become visible, as love and true brotherhood reign among all those who will be living here.

Aurelia - In my heart, I long deeply for the time when the Earth becomes a peaceful planet again. I long to experience love and true brotherhood with all sentient beings as the natural way of living. I long to see an end to human suffering and animal abuse. As I speak, I am saddened by the millions upon millions of animals abandoned and abused by insensitive humans all over the planet. This brings grief and pain to my heart.

Antharus - I know your love and I know your heart. I also know how much you love all sentient beings, all animals and those of the nature and elemental kingdoms. I also know that you will not be afraid when you see me, because your heart is open. This is why I will show myself to you as soon as you open your inner sight a little more. Though I will be at a higher frequency when you see me, I will be very physical, and you will perceive me as physical. I will lower my vibration enough for you to see me clearly, and hopefully be able to feel me by touch.

Aurelia - There is a special place I know of where I feel I might see you when taking a walk. It would be a safe place for us to meet as no one would ever see us. What do you think?

Antharus - Yes, I read your mind and I know the place you go quite often. I have occasionally accompanied you there, especially when you go alone. Though you are not aware of my presence, I send you love and protection. Have you noticed that you often fall asleep on the ground when you go there?

Aurelia - Yes.

Antharus - It is the magic, my love. As you are resting and sleeping, and your spirit leaves your body, we have a conscious etheric chat, you and I. Adama and Ahnahmar also join us quite often, and we all work on the energy fields of your physical body while it is sleeping.

Aurelia - I know that I usually feel quite good after I fall asleep there. I am aware that Adama and Ahnahmar come walking with me in the forest, but I did not know you are often present as well. So, you know them well?

Antharus - Of course. Adama and Ahnahmar were your family members in the time of Lemuria and they were my close friends also. I guarded all of you, including your children.

Aurelia - Did you go inside the mountain to Telos, or did Adama and Ahnahmar meet you on the outside?

Antharus - Well, both. When I first returned to the mountain about a year ago, I made a point to communicate telepathically with Adama, and he came out with Ahnahmar and a few others to greet me and to welcome me back. Of course, this happened at a fifth dimensional level in our light bodies. We also met in the Pleiades from time to time. Adama goes there quite often. Adama knew that I would return and he told me, while I was still in the Pleiades, that you had returned to the mountain. He said they were working more consciously with you to bring their teachings to the surface to prepare the way for their eventual emergence.

I was also invited to visit inside the mountain, which I did. I am quite tall compared to those in human form, even to those inside the mountain who are much taller than you on the surface. There are places inside the mountain especially designed to receive Light Beings such as me, some even taller, so beings of various bodily forms can meet. Many of the returning dragons met with the Lemurians and members of a few other subterranean civilizations. It was very touching for all of us to receive such a heartfelt and warm welcome back. We have a great rapport with the Lemurians. You know, not all space brothers of Light are in human form, and Inner Earth Beings are familiar with all of this. Space brothers come in all shapes, forms and colors. Some come in insect-like bodies, and many come in bodies you no longer remember, even in your wildest imaginings.

Aurelia - *I am aware of this. I read some information on that kind of thing. I don't think I would be afraid to meet a large insect-like being of Light on the street, but I am not entirely sure I must admit. I met a woman once, a few years ago, who told me that she met with a being from the stars that was about 12 feet tall and had a body that resembled the insect known as a "praying mantis." She told me that she would have been afraid to see and meet with such a being, but the love vibration exuding from him was so intense that*

149

there was no cause for fear. She met with him without being afraid. It appears that she had a multidimensional connection with that being, perhaps as part of her soul family, although she did not say.

What are your plans? Are you here to stay for a long time on the Earth now or are you planning to return to the Pleiades any time soon?

Antharus - This is not yet determined. I intend to remain here at least for the period of transition of the planet, which will be a couple of hundred years. It's possible I will remain much longer beyond that and continue my service to life on this planet.

Aurelia - *A friend of mine who is clairvoyant told me the other day that from time to time she sees a very large blue dragon flying quite elegantly at tremendous speed in the sky around the mountain. Archangel Raphael told her it was Aurelia's dragon. I assume it is you.* (Laughing)

Antharus - Indeed it is! I know her as well and that you are friends. This is why I show myself to her from time to time as I fly through the skies of this wondrous area. I am happy she was able to confirm my presence to you. You know, when your inner sight opens a bit more, you will see quite a few things in the sky around the mountain. I am only one of the many, many attractions you will be able to perceive. It will be quite interesting and wondrous. Your I AM Presence hesitates to open your inner sight at this time. There is a concern that you might become so fascinated with your "new toy" that it might compromise your mission. You have such a longing to enjoy the other dimensions, that once this opens for you, you may want to spend all your time enjoying your new perception and its magnificence, and lose interest in the chores of your daily life and mission.

Aurelia - *My friend is also excited at the thought of meeting you physically. I told her what I know about you. We have decided that one day, when we are walking together in the forest, in my "special place," as we turn the last corner before the clearing, we will both be taken by surprise and see you lying quietly in the grass, waiting for our reaction, and laughing in your heart.*

Antharus - Absolutely, you think you have it all figured out. I am a dragon, and I am not limited in any way, shape or form. I warn you that I might surprise you in other ways as well It could be the other place you often go in the hope of seeing the unicorns. Let me tell you, the unicorns know that you want to see them, and I would not be surprised if they show themselves sooner than you think.

Aurelia - *You said that many of the dragons have returned. Will they be rendering the same service to the Earth and humanity as they did in the time of Lemuria or will they be doing something else?*

Antharus - You know, things have changed on the planet in the last 100,000 years and they will soon change again, quite drastically. One can never go back, and as everything constantly changes, nothing can ever remain the same for long periods of time. Our service to life will be different this time, and it will be appropriate for the present level of evolution. It cannot be the same. I perceive that for quite some time, our service to life will be to assist your Earth Mother and humanity in rebalancing the four main elements within themselves, and then teach about the many other elements that need to be mastered. As each person gains more mastery with the elements, they assist the Earth in that stabilization as well. Nothing is separate. Everything must work together to attain perfect harmony on your planet. As a race, you have been quite destructive and inconsiderate to your planet, to the Mother who is hosting your evolution. Your planet is approaching a time of great change, and it is essential that all the elements be in balance for her safe passage.

Our service to the planet and to mankind will manifest in a more evolved way, with greater unity, love and understanding in all aspects of life. The goal is to live and work together in total harmony.

I leave you now with these thoughts and wish you good evening. I will meet you in your dream state. Call on me any time you need assistance. Know that I am never far from you and am always ready to assist you as I did in the past.

Aurelia - Thank you, my dear friend, for your love and for your return! It gives me much comfort to know you are around. I love you.

Chapter Fourteen

The Pituitary and Pineal Glands

Celestia and Ahnahmar

Greetings to all our beloved friends and family.

The shifts that are taking place in the human body are multiple. They constitute an almost complete rebuilding of the human system, and bear witness to the need for an energy matrix that supports far more energy than human bodies have been able to hold up to now. There are many teams of beings, from many galaxies, who work with the human system to modify and restructure it.

This restructuring comes through empowering human consciousness, sometimes consciously, sometimes unconsciously. For those who have given conscious intent to their personal transformation, the changes are much greater. Mankind, as a whole, is going through a global transformation, as is planet Earth. The children incarnating at this time, and in future generations, arrive with physical systems already modified in terms of DNA, organ and skeletal structure.

All organs and bodily processes are being reorganized at this time. The physical bloodstream and blood components are undergoing change. This reorganization has two components. The first is on an individual cellular level, as the core

153

of the cell is reunited with its highest level of Divinity, its GodSelf. Secondly, the energetic matrix of each cell is adapting to a higher crystalline form to allow increasingly greater amounts of pure energy to integrate with the body.

The physical structure cannot evolve without first opening to a direct experience of the Divine. The eons of separation between the physical third dimensional body and the full spectrum of Divine Love is over. The process of transformation now unfolding must include the Divine aspect, otherwise cosmic alteration through divine grace cannot be made.

In the initial stages of this empowering process, the pineal and pituitary glands play significant roles. The pineal gland has long been the organ of intuition and knowingness in the human body.

It is through the pineal gland that connection is made with the etheric world.

In communities that exist in the fifth and higher dimensions, however, the pineal gland fulfills an even greater role. It is, in fact, the organ of communication through mental telepathy, just as the throat chakra has filled that role through the vocal cords in third dimensional bodies.

Many individuals with highly developed pineal glands have lived in the third dimension. Some of these individuals make up the ranks of channels and psychics who have populated earlier metaphysical literature and mystery schools. There are other sentient races on Earth today, namely dolphins and whales, who communicate through use of this gland.

The work being done today with the pineal gland is global, and all humans on Earth are experiencing an increase in intuition and non-verbal contact with other humans and realms. For some, this shift is disconcerting; for others, it is the answer to a prayer. For all, valuable contact is now readily available with the totality of self and various forms of spiritual information such as the Akashic records and the living libraries that exist in the etheric realms of the planet. In fact, the term channel or psychic will soon cease to exist, as all will have the ability to communicate and connect with all realms. Contemplate living in a world where everyone is spiritually awakened. We are grateful for those who have volunteered to serve humanity as true channels for the light; this service greatly contributes to the spiritual awakening of humanity.

Channeling, which has grown increasingly in the last few decades, can be compared to a lighthouse illuminating the way for a sleeping humanity. Nevertheless, we see this service as only a temporary phase in the spiritual awakening of mankind. The time is soon coming when everyone will become their own "lighthouse" and regain the skills and gifts that already reside within the heart. In a few years, those who remain incarnated on the planet will all be fully telepathic. Those who have assisted humanity as channels will continue their service in a different way.

This increase of activity in the pineal gland corresponds to the increase of vibration in the sacred heart chakra. These two energy centers, which work together, allow the increase of pineal activity to proceed in the vibration of Divine Grace. Without the balance of love, compassion and true respect for the sanctity of others, the increased amount of information could be manipulated by the human ego and the course of evolution could be stunted once again. In all civilizations that communicate non-verbally, fully supporting and surrendering to the greatest good of the whole is essential. There must be the highest levels of inter-personal nurturing and truth-telling. All must honor the privacy of the individual heart for this level of communication to be truly open and effective.

The information received by the pineal gland must always

be validated by the knowingness of the heart. In this way, the True Mind is the servant of the True Heart, and the opportunity for community and Divine Grace on the planet is nourished.

The pituitary gland holds another role in the evolution of the human body. The human endocrine system has been the repository for many of the limitations placed on humans during the experience of duality and separation. In truth, the rise of auto-immune diseases has a direct correlation to the long-term grief that many a soul has experienced through these feelings of separation. But the pituitary gland is now being released from its limitations, and the physical body will once again be able to regenerate and repair itself to the fullest extent of its energies.

Again, the energy of conscious intent provides the starting point for these changes. The enhanced organs of the human body will continue to respond most powerfully when informed by the consciousness of the individual. The human system is a complex one, and two organs cannot be held in separation from the others. Much work must be done on an individual basis to detoxify and nourish all organs of the body.

Communication with the organ elementals to determine what is the best course for each individual is a recommended step. Consultation with an energy specialist, healer or body worker is highly suggested. There are new energy tools making their way to the surface, all of which will alter the way you treat physical, mental and emotional imbalances. Seek these out and utilize them. Now is the time for all to recognize, at the deepest levels, what a true gift the human body is. Your ancient scriptures that refer to the body as a temple of the Divine were accurate. Your conscious participation in the healing and transformation of the body is what will allow you to create bodies you wish to live in.

Loving your body as a Divine repository of spirit is equally as important as loving the totality of your spirit.

Only when this is accomplished on a global level will the changes that you all desire be made to your food resources and global healing modalities. Even now, tools and substances with great ability to heal and rebuild are beginning to enter mainstream consciousness and markets. It is your continued support and your ability to trust in new forms of healing which will allow this shift to take place across the planet.

The wondrous temples of rejuvenation and healing of old that you so wish for and envision in your future, are in fact here now. They still exist in the consciousness of their original builders and designers. They exist in the energetic memories of those of you who experienced them in other times. Though they may have been destroyed in their third dimensional aspect, they still exist in the higher dimensions, Their original intention and purposes are greatly expanded for use in this present time, and you can draw on these energies without great difficulty or monetary expense. All you need to do is quiet your mind, open your heart and set your intention to connect and experience these energies for your own healing. Allow the process to take place. As long as you allow yourself each day to spend enough time breathing and infusing these energies into your body, the process will be initiated and you will witness extraordinary results.

Together, simply through the power of intention and surrender to Divine Grace, you can magnetize these energies into your auric field at any time. The benefits of these energies can be recreated in the present. The form may not mirror the original, but the energy is the same. The crystalline matrix computer may replace the temple of crystal, but the action is the same.

Recognize the healers and tools in your midst and support them. In times to come, you may wish to recreate the temples, but without first recognizing the ancient tools as they are today, and without first accepting yourselves as you are today, these potentials cannot manifest. Heaven exists around you now, on this planet. It may seem to be true in only little ways, but by giving recognition to all who are working to create this paradise, you support the potential for a global paradise. Do not suffer over what has been, but celebrate instead what is re-emerging.

Be gentle with yourselves, for who else can better love you than you?

Chapter Fifteen

The Spirit of Community

Celestia

Celestia is an elder in Telos and a counselor to the High Council. She is also the sister of Adama. She works with the children of Telos and acts as an instrument of their interaction with the elders.

Welcome home, dear ones! It is so wonderful to see you gathered here. Your love brings tears to our eyes. We perceive you in the full radiance of your light bodies and in the beauty of who you are.

There are so many more of you who are now awakening to the truth of your divinity. We rejoice to witness an increase in the number of gatherings taking place within our energies. The number of souls participating in these sharings is expanding. The intensity of the Light generated is becoming more visible, even in the darkest corners of the surface of the planet.

We have held the space and the energy here in Mount Shasta for a long time. A great number of you have lived several lifetimes in this area, both in Telos and on the surface, helping to hold this energy. Most of you have aspects of yourselves living inside the mountain and in other cities

159

inside the Earth. For us, it is wonderful beyond measure to see you now, in your physical incarnation, because you are the ones who are bringing about the great shift that is so needed on this planet.

I would like to introduce you to the children of Telos and other Lemurian cities throughout the Earth. They have eagerly awaited their time to connect more consciously with you, because they want to teach you more about playing and having fun again. So much of your journey now is about reopening your heart and rediscovering those things that, as a child, brought you joy. It is essential that you open your imagination and fully envision the paradise that you wish to create and experience on the surface. The children are here, with open hearts, to show you how to create the world you desire through your visions and the power of your imagination.

The children of Telos would be happy to be guides and assist you to lighten your way.

You can contact them right now. These children have volunteered to become your emissaries to "playland" and will stay with you for as long as you wish. All you need to do is begin to communicate with them from your heart. They may come to you in your dream time, or you may recognize them around you right now. As many of you who are clairvoyant will soon discover, Telosian children have much longer lifespans than those who live on the surface. The child that comes to play with you may be 200 years old in your timeframe. Do not be surprised if the image of the playmate that appears to you is not what you expected.

Trust the images your inner sight brings and trust the messages you are hearing from the children of Telos. They are here to reintroduce you to these parts of yourself that may be shut down, and to that magic of imagination that allows you to create anything you want and to know that it is absolutely real. Imagination is our mechanism for creation, but it is not "unreal," as many languages on the surface define it. You are now rediscovering just how real imagination can be and to what extent it creates wonders or painful challenges, in accordance with the thoughts and emotions you entertain.

In Telos, we create by imagining what we want, and then project, in energetic terms, the potentials that manifest tangibly what we have imagined.

Imagination is our key to manifestation. We do so by blending the masculine inspiration of the Divine with the energies of the feminine that nurtures and holds these inspirations or imaginings until they become manifest. As the consciousness of incarnated beings on the Earth's surface embraces more and more of the Divine Feminine, these principles of manifestation will once again become activated. As the nurturing soul of Earth is recognized and allowed to re-establish herself in nature and in society, the true inspiration of the Divine will express itself in oneness, in your daily lives and through the building of community.

You are reawakening to the concepts of true community through your exploration and reconnection with us, your family in Telos. Whenever any of you come together to work, play, study, or meditate, in Mount Shasta or any other region of the planet, you form the spirit of community. These communities may appear as a temporary event, but they are not.

The energy that is generated from each gathering connects with the energy of other similar gatherings, and a larger community is formed energetically, outside of time and space. These connections are formed with the souls who participate, and the energy of community then lights a pathway for more to join in.

In Telos, the paradigm we operate within is one of total

co-operation and complete sharing of resources. Everyone is taken care of; we share our time and energies to accomplish this. This most important principle will eventually be adopted by the societies and governments on the surface. In this way, you can begin to demonstrate and live the Telosian model of community as a harmonious gathering of energies.

New societal lifestyles are already developing in this country, and many of you are now awakening to the true promise and ideal of community. Many more are beginning to feel the seeds of new ideas and ways of living sprouting in your consciousness. This is one of the most important steps that must be taken to help bring this vibration to the surface and the planet to a whole new level.

The fifth dimensional vibration that sustains us in Telos is the energy of a community of the heart.

We have taken the steps to create the world we want to live in, and now we offer ourselves as guides to show you the way. The community of the heart is a place where everyone is in complete harmonic resonance. Any need or want is communicated telepathically and then met by the community as a whole. It is a community where you will find no lack or suffering because the communal heart energy of compassion and nurturing is always present. These are the concepts we want to share with you. You are already experiencing this to some extent in Mount Shasta where so many individuals share themselves on so many levels with those around them. When a great need occurs and many people are required, there are many who step in to share the load.

We ask that within every aspect of your selves and every aspect of your hearts, you begin to expand your consciousness to include the concept of true community. Know that you are surrounded by beings who love you. You may not know all of them consciously yet, but you are beginning to recognize them. You are beginning to connect with every being you come into contact with and you are beginning to form community.

Part of my service in Telos is working with potentials; let me share some with you now. Communities are going to form around Mount Shasta in the next couple of years. People will come together for the purpose of creating a role model for the establishment of other communities on the planet. They will be examples of how humans can live in the spirit of true brotherhood, compassion and cooperation.

Openings have already begun to take place on the planet to prepare the way for our emergence from our Inner Earth cities, and the harmonizing of our lives together with yours. A portal has begun to open in recent months encompassing many of the Western states of the United States, including the area of Mount Shasta. It is through this portal that the first Inner Earth beings have already begun to emerge and create, with their vibration, a passageway through which others will eventually follow.

There are passageways that are being cleared in the Mount Shasta area that relate directly to Telos. There are star-gates that are in the first stages of reactivation, as well as some that are already in full use around the mountain. The gatekeepers, who etherically maintain these energies, are beginning to awaken to their roles and are coming together in greater numbers in your dimension.

This work has always been done multi-dimensionally, but your awareness of it has been veiled. Soon this work will be recognized worldwide, and many around you who have always discounted this kind of spiritual work will step forward to take on roles you cannot imagine at this time.

We share this with you in order to encourage you as you journey forward; we know that speaking of these wonders to come brings you hope. We ask you to live your lives in this new awareness and experience your evolution with that hope, with that heart, because potential miracles exist all around you. It is up to you to open yourself to them. If each of you would speak to one person that you don't already know, and open up your heart to him or her in the same way that you do with us, the surface community of Earth could be born very quickly. This sharing from the heart would expand with each additional contact that is made between citizens and neighbors around the planet. How wondrous that could be!

> *True intimacy occurs when two souls can nurture each other with authenticity, spontaneity and truth-telling.*

Do not be afraid to open yourself to another, for nothing during this time of great awakening and transformation is to be avoided. There is nothing that can truly hinder you on your path of evolution, other than limitation. Do not hesitate to open the door into your soul's depths and explore the fullness of your experiences and emotions. Do not hesitate, in a loving and supportive way, to hold that same space for another. There is much clearing that must take place, much purification, before you will be able to enter the higher vibration you so desire and form communities of the heart.

Begin to form communities of two. Reach out to each other in ways that you have not trusted before. Be witnesses, for each other, of the incredible soul paths that each of you has traveled. Only when we can open ourselves to each other in this way are we able to experience greater heart and soul bondings within community.

Call on us as at any time. We will listen to you without judgment or condition. Set the intention in your heart to fully open to the vibration in which we live, so that you can begin to experience it daily. The more you recognize and integrate this vibration in your day-to-day activities, the quicker the vibration of the surface will rise. We are always there for you. Please call on us to be at your side; we cannot emphasize this enough. Most importantly, enjoy the new energy, the new vibrations that are transforming your very soul and your planet day by day. Enjoyment will speed this process along with a magic that is only now being rediscovered.

Call on the children of Telos to come and play with you. Call on them to join you and share their innate sense of enjoyment and pleasure in the simple act of being. When you are in your darkest states and the struggle seems almost too much to bear is when you need them the most. Their joy and playfulness, their creative and imaginative perceptions of the world around them and around you will open your heart again to the magical child that resides within you. Laugh, giggle and joke with them. Look through their eyes and clear away the residue of despair from your own; they will cheer you up when nothing else seems to work. They'll bring groups of kids and have parties in your house.

The children like to visit you to gain a greater understanding of what it is that you are experiencing on the surface, in your journey in the third dimensional reality. This is a part of their education, and they have readily volunteered to meet you as a necessary part of their schooling.

We love you more than we can express. Once again, welcome home, my beloved friends.

The love of our Earth Mother,
And the willingness with which
She offers to take our pain,
Endows us each and every day
With the strength to continue our journey.
- Angelina

Chapter Sixteen

Emissaries of Lemuria,
Awaken to Your Ancient Memories

Hyrham, a member of the scientific community of Telos

Greetings, my beloved friends, this is Hyrham.

All of you reading these words have connections to Telos. You have all had lifetimes in Lemuria, and you are now among the brothers and sisters who shared those lifetimes with you. We ask you to come together whenever possible and reach out to those memories. We invite you to ask for and gather information to reawaken the recollections of your ancient past. We ask you to send your energies out in search of connections, past and present, to each other and to us as well. Open your inner awareness and speak to us in your higher mind; then listen within the deep recesses of your heart for the reply.

Each time you open up and trust your own sense of who you were then, and who you are now, you are opening to more levels of your own multi-dimensional self. As this trust builds, we are able to communicate with you on deeper and more varied levels. More layers of memory and understanding can be explored and shared with you. You are all awakening to your true Self and divine identity, and as you awaken, you will find that there is so much more to embrace.

167

You are emissaries.

You are emissaries of Lemuria and of a vibration that is creating openings on this planet in ways that we never knew were possible. You are emissaries for aspects of your totality, and you have evolved through eons of incarnations on this planet. It is time, dear ones, to incorporate into oneness all these aspects of yourself again, in this lifetime, in these bodies. The more you can open up to and embrace all of the aspects of you, the more you will access the experience and wisdom you gained in each incarnation. Each time you clear and transform energies that keep you from opening to the totality of yourself, the more you will experience your soul's joy and understanding of the paradise that this planet can return to again.

When you travel, share this vibration with everyone that you meet. When you walk down the street, the people who are smiling at you are brothers and sisters; you know them. In the lifetimes that we have shared together on this planet, there exists a oneness we are all beginning to understand and embrace once again.

Mount Shasta is a giant heart that is beaming love to everyone and everything on the planet.

She is literally a physical incarnation of Source energies. Our Sacred Mountain represents the heart of Mother Earth and the love She feels for us all. Wherever you are, you can connect with Her. Feel that love and let it flow out through you to others. When you are in close proximity to the mountain, you will feel yourself activated by her energies, and you will carry that bond through all of your incarnations.

All of you who journey to Mount Shasta have returned here because you have experienced that bond in prior lifetimes. It is this bond in the heart that supported the creation of Telos within Her energies at the time of the fall of Lemuria.

We encourage you to spend time here, and then carry these energies to the rest of the planet.

I am Hyrham, a scientist in Telos. I am currently working as a member of a team of scientists participating in a program of several years, to measure the energies around Mount Shasta. We are assessing what is needed for us inside the mountain to join with you on the outside as one civilization.

I am a member of the team that has been monitoring these vibrations since 2001. We intend to continue our program in an ever-increasing circle around and beyond the mountain. The circle currently extends out from the mountain in a circumference of approximately six to seven miles, with a second circle approximately 20 miles. We measure your vibration as individuals, and that of the planet as a whole. We also measure your intention and that of all beings, taking note of who is capable of recognizing and moving into the vibration of Lemuria. We monitor these vibrations with anticipation because we are just as eager as you are, if not more so, to be together again.

Our understanding of your energies is different than your understanding of ours. We have a greater range of perception from which to understand you. We can see your energy field as well as the physical body. We see your light body, as well as your multi-dimensional and "future" aspects. We can see many more pieces of you than you can see of us at this time. The people of Telos, who follow our progress and anticipate its eventual outcome, wish you to know how important your intention and recognition of all multiple timelines is to this potential. The work you have done to recognize and clear ancient trauma from these timelines has been so important in creating a doorway not only for Mount Shasta and the planet, but for your Higher Selves to work through. This opening will allow you to integrate all aspects of yourselves and to recognize them as we do. You will even recognize "future" aspects of yourself, which is here in full participation.

169

What we are speaking of in terms of the future has already happened, and these aspects of your selves have already played their roles. The goal now is to merge all of these timelines together vibrationally and experience the joy of reunion that has already been created and already exists around us.

You may be called to venues and gatherings of people interested in Lemuria and other metaphysical topics. As each group, large or small, comes together on the planet, whether made up of those formerly together in Lemuria or from the time of Atlantis, the vibration shared in that time and space is recognized and experienced, even if for just a moment. Much understanding is gained from that recognition. Soon these groups will begin to come together and harmonize for an even greater understanding. The new wisdom that each group opens to will create harmonious purpose and cooperation among all people; this is the type of loving energy that will birth the new Lemuria and the new Earth.

Our past is full of non-cooperation and discord and the painful lessons that flow from them. We have lived through the many permutations of human experience created by duality, separation and disharmony. Now is the time to remember and re-experience the vibration of harmony and to gain new understanding of the potentials for pure creative energy that this form of synthesized intent can bring. It is a time for all beings on the planet, in all dimensions, to re-invent themselves through the energies of unconditional love and harmony, and explore the expansion of this vibration on our planet.

Inherent in this return to harmony, however, is the organic process of detoxification that will occur in your physical and emotional bodies as new levels of love are re-introduced. As each of you re-integrates your Divine essence and reestablishes your connection to Divine Source, you will experience great shifts in your mental, physical and emotional structure. This is to be expected as you are transmuting much old energy on a cellular level. We will do as much as we can to support you through this process.

The citizens of Telos want you to know that your journey now very much mirrors the journey they themselves took when they created their new world within the Earth following the fall of Lemuria. The cataclysm that we experienced shifted us in the same ways you are being asked to shift now. The children of Telos yearn, even more than the elders, to venture outside the mountain, to learn about their brothers and sisters and to experience the world they have heard so much about. There must be a merging of energies now. When the opening comes, we will journey out into your dimension in physical form. As we bring our vibration closer to you, so must you move your vibration closer to ours to make this happen.

Soon, we will merge our vibrations together in a new dimension. All energies, from within and beyond this planet, are focused on creating this transformation. We ask you now to hold this same intention. Each time you recognize or remember who you have been, who we have been, and that we will be together again, you activate your intention. Each time you open your heart to the mountain, to the elementals, to the pictures we paint for you in the sky, to the ships that visit you sending you love and energy through the lenticular clouds, you activate your intention. Verbalize your goals and ours, and simply trust!

The assessment program will begin to culminate around the year 2009. Plans will be made at that time to begin the opening of dimensions, for some of us to come out, and some of you to come inside the Earth. With each passing year, many more portals will open and the visitations of those who can travel the most easily between the dimensions will begin. They will prepare the energy pathways for those who will follow later. Many of you are involved energetically with these portal activities. Many of you have multi-dimensional aspects currently residing in Telos or other Lemurian cities who play dynamic roles in these activities. Open yourselves to these energies and begin to incorporate them into the aspect of yourself incarnated on the surface. Honor the messages you receive and share them with others, as this too will build an energy of hope and trust for what is to come. The planetary shift right now is accelerating at a very great rate, and at the end of a three-year period, there will be greater access to some of the cities of the Earth's interior. Call on us and ask questions. We are here to guide you.

Questions from an Audience in Mount Shasta

The Telosians are multi-dimensional, as is the city of Telos. Did the Telosians phase-shift the entire city inside Mount Shasta at the time of the last volcanic eruption of Mount Shasta in the 1700's?

The city inside Mount Shasta today is not the same energetically as the one prior to the last volcanic eruption. There was a dimensional shift at that time. The energies of the eruption shifted major portals and energetic spots around the mountain that were used for communication and travel. The etheric energies were not affected, but the physical shifting of the Earth, in terms of her needs and meridian channels, made it necessary for the Telosians to reconstruct and redirect various energy channels and portals through and around the mountain.

The heart of the city of Telos is located very deep within the mountain and is shielded dimensionally in such a way that it was not affected by the eruption. Some of the energetic structures around the mountain that allow access to the inside were greatly affected. Some portals were closed and new ones created in different locations. Some portals needed energetic repair and still exist in their original locations. We do not foresee this type of disruption happening again in the future. We understand Earth energies and the need for the volcanic release that took place. We were forewarned of the eruption and were able to make plans prior to the disturbance.

What can we do to help so that the Telosians can come out of the mountain and we can be allowed in?

First and foremost is your intention. It is knowing that this will happen, and committing yourself so completely that you live these energies and bring the vibration into your daily life and the life of others around you. There will be ever-increasing changes taking place on the Earth that may make you feel you are being thrown out of the vibration you wish to hold, or even that you want to respond in other ways. You will soon witness and experience the effects of the clearing going on within the emotional body of both the Earth Mother and the civilizations on her surface. You will also encounter new levels of anger and violence on the surface. Recognize that this is part of the healing crisis you are all going through. There is much that must be stripped away and detoxified to allow the new vibration to come in.

Hold onto the energies that reside in the knowingness and love of your heart. Commit to the new energies of light flooding your planet at this time with all aspects of your being. Understand, as your physical body and emotions experience trauma, sadness or overwhelm, that your totality is still living the vibration of love and compassion. Know in your heart that you can connect back in with that vibration at any moment.

Ask for help from your guides and angels, from your family here in Telos and from your Star brothers who are here to assist.

Allow all of us who are here to support you, to hold you

in our embrace of love. Allow all of your feelings to be released without condition or judgment. Give your energies permission to move again and flow with Divine Grace. Ask each and every day for the release of all energies that block you from recognizing the totality of who you are in this moment.

Your journey here in physical form, at a time when the planet is transiting from a third to fifth dimensional existence, requires that you live fully as the physical and emotional human being you are. The goal is to learn to live consciously in an increasing level of vibration at all times, as if your life were a continuous walking meditation. Voice your intention to recognize and maintain full awareness of the totality of who you are and the vibration in which you choose to live.

If you can begin by simply hearing and/or seeing through us, through the mirror that we provide, you will always have a place to go when you feel disillusioned, disconnected or confused. Use us as your mirror until such time as you see and trust yourself completely. Know that we can help you on your journey and hold the vibration of love and grace for you. Allow yourself to return it whenever you call us by expressing your intent.

Adama, Ahnahmar and many others hold classes every night in Telos. You may ask, before going to sleep and in your dreams to come here and receive teachings, healings and reconnect with your own remembrance. Set your intention to remember, upon returning to normal consciousness, all you have experienced, so that what has been revealed to you in Telos may be remembered in your waking hours as well.

Most important is that you give yourself permission to experience, remember and learn, without judgment and without critical analysis.

You are moving into a higher vibration when you make these journeys to Telos, a vibration of trust and harmony. The information that you desire can only be shared through this energetic field. A channel must be opened from our hearts to yours and this can only happen in a vibration of trust and unconditional love. We will bring our vibration to meet yours from a place of love and openness. You cannot prejudge or set expectations for what will happen in these meetings. You must simply open yourself as a conduit to accept with grace all that we have to give you.

You may speak to any of us at any time. Ask your questions and listen. The answer may come to you as a tone, music, a voice or simply as a knowingness. Do not let your mind analyze the answer. Simply recognize and allow the awareness to grow. As your awareness expands, the conversations you have with us will become as commonplace as those you have with the physical brothers and sisters around you. Give yourself permission to do this now.

What are some of the tools or healing methods you will share with us from Telos in the future?

The temples of rejuvenation and healing in the area of Mount Shasta will be re-activated and re-consecrated for these purposes. Energies from the Earth and the elementals will flow once again into them.

New healing and rejuvenation techniques will emerge comprised of two elements. First, rituals of intent will be initiated which fully engage the energy of the individual in the process of self-healing. The second element will be tools that utilize light and sound. These tools will be crystalline in nature, as the human form is now returning to its true crystalline matrix. Some of these tools will be in the form of helmets and full body chambers, similar to the sarcophagi that you remember from Ancient Egypt. They will be made of intensely prismatic crystal material.

Sound is a conductor for the energies of healing and renewal. Light represents all the various frequencies we can resonate with. Sound penetrates dimensional layers and carries the light or frequency needed for healing, through the various bodies—physical, emotional, etheric and mental.

Crystal has a very refined ability to transmit both sound and light. The healer, and sometimes the individual who is being healed, will work with multi-dimensional toning, through a combination of voice, musical instruments such as crystal flutes or bowls, and angelic and elemental energies. All these tones will then be transferred through a "crystal sound magnifier" which refines the multi-tones into one multi-level sound that accesses the entire sound spectrum simultaneously as "conscious sound." This conscious sound then entrains the space around it to act as a conduit for healing light frequencies. These appear as colors beyond the current spectrum of human sight. In this way, healing will take place in all bodies simultaneously.

There will be smaller tools as well. Some will be worn on the body and others will be carried. Some will be used in daily meditation or simply placed around the individual's home. Many of you already use these types of tools today. These new devices will be more refined than the ones you already have. Some tools will be created for an individual at the time of incarnation and will stay with that person throughout the life span. Others will be shared among family members to hold the harmonic of a family group.

The understanding of and relationship to crystals and to the full spectrum of sound and light frequencies will be taught to children in the first levels of schooling. Most construction of buildings, homes and temples will be done with pure crystalline material that has been consecrated with sacred tones, allowing it to hold a constant healing and harmonizing vibration within the structure itself.

What can I do as an individual to raise my vibration?

Each of you who so desires may have a guide in Telos assigned to you. Simply make the request and connect through the heart. Ask to meet your guide and communicate with him or her on a regular basis. Use your guide as a tuning fork for the vibration you are trying to harmonize with.

Each of you also has individual responsibilities in terms of your own clearing. You have all come here to clear energies that impede you from reaching a vibration and a level of enjoyment in incarnation that is new to you. Each time you clear old energy or heal an old emotional pattern, you create openings for new and expanded energies to come in. In addition, the clearing provides a release for everyone on the planet. Each of you holds a different piece of group consciousness that you volunteered to clear for humanity and for the planet. This is an important task. It is time to recognize it and acknowledge the trust we hold in you to accomplish this. You are not in Telos at this moment, and there is a good reason for this.

You have all volunteered to be here, in physical incarnation, to help in the healing of the planet and in the freeing of humanity from the consciousness of pain and separation. Your work is here, and the vibration you have agreed to bring to this planet must be experienced here.

Those who come behind you are looking to you to clear the way. Each time you clear grief and trauma from your emotional body, you also clear it from the Earth Mother's emotional body. All of us in the various dimensions are here to support you in this task, as we honor the time and energy that this journey takes. It is our great pleasure to shower you with love while you do this important work.

In the distant past, there was a greater understanding of

177

how we exist within the universe. You understood how to connect and operate within the sphere, the flow of the God Source. You understood the grids of energy in which we operate and the matrices of all the bodies. This knowledge is now being reclaimed. The more you understand and experience this knowledge again and incorporate it into your present Earth-plane existence, the more you step into reclaiming your true divinity in this time and in this body. This is indeed a time of great awakening and we celebrate with you.

We love you with the totality of our beings. We send you our love in harmony, in cooperation, in colors, sounds and in songs. Thank you for your loving attention.

Chapter Seventeen

Final Message in Honor of the Telosians

Master Saint Germain

Greetings, my dearest friends.

I am Saint Germain, the guardian of the Violet Flame and the one who champions your victory. It has been this very precious flame of violet frequency that initiated and ignited the ascension energies for this planet so long ago.

I am here at this time with Adama, the Lemurian Council of Telos and a large gathering of your Lemurian family and other beings of the Light Realm. It is time, dear ones, for your Lemurian brothers and sisters of Telos to be honored and acknowledged for the wonderful work they have done for this planet for so long. They are the ones, along with others, who have diligently kept the focus of the Ascension Flame for the planet during the last 12,000 years, while the surface populations busied themselves warring against each other.

Had it not been for your wondrous and dedicated Lemurian family beneath Mount Shasta, and other cities of the Agartha Network, who nurtured the flame of ascension on your behalf, the potentials you are now manifesting may not have happened. The law of balance between receiving and giving requires that a certain emanation of light energy be generated and mirrored back to the Creator by a receiving planet and its inhabitants, in recognition of and gratitude for the tremendous amount of Love and Light energy sent from Source. This is a cosmic law. For many thousands of years, the surface populations of Earth reflected very little light back to Father/Mother God in exchange for all the Light and Love they received in support of their third dimensional experience.

The Ascension Flame and the Violet Flame, beloved ones, may have a different frequency, but they both lead to ascension, complementing each other effectively. They are related. Both are flames of freedom in their own frequency. Any energy expressed as less than divine love can be transmuted by the Violet Flame.

At some point, all humanity choosing ascension as the next step will be given the opportunity to present themselves to their God Presence and to the Office of the Christ, headed by the masters Maitreya and Sananda. The necessary initiations will then be presented to you, in your daily life, to prepare you for that sacred event. At the time of your ascension, your consciousness and life stream will be drenched in the fires of the Ascension Flame, and any energy still vibrating in less than pure love will be completely consumed by this flame. Then, only pure light will remain. This is how, my friends, you will embrace your eternal birthright of living your life as pure beings of love and light, enjoying eternal peace, bliss, immortality and limitlessness.

If you have integrated appropriate levels of Love and Light in your causal body and in all your subtle bodies, you will be totally transformed as an ascended master by this process. Those who have not yet reached this level of evolution will have the opportunity for additional incarnations to walk the path of love and reach the level of ascension you desire.

What would happen to a soul who has not garnered enough love and light in their causal body to be put through the process of the Ascension Flame?

Well, my friends, if a soul is not ready to embrace such a process, the end result could mean the dissolution of the soul. The Ascension Flame consumes, by its nature, all that is anti-light and anti-love. All that is held in the soul must be embraced and allowed to breathe in the vibration of understanding. All must be accepted, recognized and allowed before this final step is taken. Otherwise, there would be nothing left of that soul were it allowed to go through the process before embracing the initiations of unconditional love and light.

The opportunity for ascension for everyone has never been so easily available to mankind as it is at this time. Because the Lemurians have kept the "vigil" on your behalf for so long, they have smoothed the way for all of you.

It was our Lemurian friends, these precious souls, who, on a daily basis have reflected the Light back to God on behalf of mankind for thousands of years.

This is why the seat of the Ascension Flame, the headquarters of ascension for the planet, is now in Telos. The great pyramid of Giza held the Ascension Flame energy for a long time on this planet. Giza still holds an important ascension focus in Egypt, but the Telosians are now in charge of this Herculean project and have shouldered this mantle for the planet. They work very closely with Serapis Bey, the Chohan of the Ascension Flame; their work together is a co-creation in service to mankind. The Lemurians had sufficient population to keep the Ascension Flame burning bright on behalf of humanity until this day.

Thousands of years ago, many of us had not yet ascended. I, Saint Germain, had not yet ascended. The Lemurians took on the task as way-showers for us all. In the Light realm, we bow to them as our elder brothers and sisters and deeply honor them for their love, courage and wonderful service to this planet.

On behalf of the various brotherhoods of the Light Realm, I wish to honor Adama and his divine complement Galatia of Telos, who is incarnated on the surface as Aurelia, for their long service to mankind and to this planet. They are the original "Father and Mother of humanity," your biblical figures known as Adam and Eve. The story of Adam and Eve that most of you are familiar with reflects very little, if any, of the real truth of the wondrous story of that first chapter of Lemurian history. Perhaps this will be material for a future publication, as the true story of Adam and Eve would certainly enlighten mankind. You have not been taught the real story by the historians and scholars of your world.

"Adama and Galatia-Aurelia, we all love you so very much, and on behalf of all beings of the Light Realm, we express our deep gratitude for your millions of years of service to mankind, on and within the Earth."

For most on the surface, Lemuria, the cradle of enlightened civilizations on this planet, has been the mother-land of your own evolution. For hundreds of thousands of years, you evolved there in a state of paradise and bliss until, as a collective, you chose to experience separation and duality. Now the consciousness of Lemuria, in its full splendor and glory, is opening Her Heart again, to bring you "home" to the land and love of your heart. The energies of Lemuria and her people, your former family, is imprinted in the very cellular structure of your DNA, your cellular memory. Lemuria, as it exists today, is the heritage you have been seeking lifetime after lifetime.

I, Saint Germain, say to all of you, "Reach for Lemuria's vibration and find the lost paradise within yourselves. The doorway for your return has remained within your heart; it was never removed. Reactivate those treasures within the Self and you will discover your Lemurian family awaiting your return and ready to meet you half way."

I, Saint Germain, am always at your side, and I love you so very much. I champion your victory through your ascension. Though my main focus is elsewhere, I spend much time in Mt. Shasta, Telos and the New Lemuria, in full support of the Lemurian mission for the ascension and restoration of the planet and of humanity to "Divine Grace." Though I have had several incarnations in leadership roles in Atlantis, I am also a Lemurian! Join me there in the vibration of love and harmony!

The Channeling of Adama
By Aurelia Louise Jones

(Publisher's Note: Due to the passing of Aurelia Louise Jones in July, 2009, the material in this chapter has been edited to reflect her concerns about channeled information that remains pertinent today. Adama continues to communicate through channels around the world and it is up to each person to determine from within their own heart the authenticity of the messages received.)

At the present time, there are an increasing number of people claiming to channel Adama. On the Internet, all kinds of messages are floating around in his name. In some cases, I know these to be authentic, while others are not. Because the name of Adama is written at the bottom of a message does not necessarily mean that it comes from him.

I take no responsibility for any information published by other people in the name of Adama or Ahnahmar; the information may or may not be authentic.

Since the publishing of the Telos books Volumes 1, 2 and 3, there are a number of people who state they have become channels for Adama and for Ahnahmar. All kinds of channeled information is now circulating on the Internet and elsewhere, especially in newsgroups, published in the name of Adama. Some are sweet and appear to be coming from the heart, while others are simply erroneous and do not carry the Lemurian vibration. Unfortunately, this is confusing for serious truth seekers and for those who have not yet developed enough discernment and clarity to distinguish the difference between what is authentic and what is not.

Adama is often asked questions by people desiring to gain a level of discernment regarding channeled information

*written in his name. People want to know who they can
trust and how to tell the difference between those who are
truly channeling him and those who are simply channeling themselves or other entities of lesser vibration posing as
Adama. It is not always easy, even for me, to discern who
is authentic and who is not, or to judge the intentions of
others, as judgments are always traps. Each person must
exercise their own discernment, and thus gain their stripes
in spiritual mastery.*

Here is what Adama has to say:

"According to Divine Law, it is the Master who chooses its
channel and not the incarnated person. One must wait for
an official invitation from a Master from the other side of
the veil in order to channel that Master. No master is allowed to speak through a person unless this Master receives
permission from the Creator Himself. The candidate to
channel for a Master must have passed through spiritual
initiations required by hierarchy over a period of several
lifetimes to be granted such a privilege. Those wanting to
channel me without the proper preparation and without a
specific invitation to do so, beyond offering the occasional
message to a small group or to give comfort to someone in
need, may be presenting an illusion, because I am not always present or willing to communicate.

"There is a risk of our teachings becoming distorted and
biased at the hands of those who have not yet received the
initiations and inner training. It often creates an invitation
to those who have a personal agenda to corrupt our teachings with non-truths. Our original teachings are no longer
in existence, because they have been corrupted again and
again by those without the clarity or integrity of intention
the teachings require.

"Our teachings carry the Lemurian consciousness, origi-
nating from Divine Source. Distortion is always a concern,

especially by those wanting to profit from a subject that has become popular. This causes much confusion in the hearts and souls of those we are trying to reach, and those who are truly trying to reach us.

"If I am present at one of your gatherings, it does not mean that it is always appropriate for me to bring forth a message. We wish the hearts of those desiring communication to be in touch with the highest integrity of Lemurian energies, and not someone posing as Ahnahmar, myself or others from Telos.

"There are those who have used my image and have written sales pitches in my name to promote their products and their scams. Please know, dear ones, that I do not participate in such endeavors and that I am certainly not a salesman for those without integrity.

"All channeled messages not authentic hold a vibration of personal agenda and can become spiritual traps. Be aware, my friends, that many of those who contributed to the destruction of both continents are also incarnated at this time, and some of them are determined to stop the Light from coming in. They want to stop the Lemurian emergence in any way they can. They will often disguise themselves as angels of Light coming to your rescue and make you all kinds of alluring offers. I ask you not to be deceived and always check with the discernment in your heart.

"This time, my friends, the stakes are too high for the planet and for your own personal evolution. Be aware that you will be confronted with tests of discernment in more ways than one. Become sovereign in your divine powers as masters.

"Know it is always my pleasure to connect and speak with you directly in your heart. Sometimes I am present in your gatherings radiating my energy and my love to all of you, but I remain silent and unnoticed. For us, the energy we bring is often more important to your transformation than the words. Many times words can be limiting. I ask you to receive and cherish these precious moments, holding what is shared deep within your heart. You do not have to share on the Internet and elsewhere everything you receive from us. Most transmissions are directed and appropriate for those present at that time and not intended for public dissemination.

"I also want to add that in Telos, I am the one who has volunteered to enter the public eye on the surface. The others, especially Ahnahmar, have not chosen to do so because their time has not yet come. Ahnahmar does not wish to have his image commercialized or go public other than in an occasional channeling here and there.

"Ahnahmar and I are certainly not interested in bringing forth messages through those beings who do not embody the integrity and transparency of the Lemurian vibration.

"We are happy to give you personal messages when your heart tunes in to ours in your meditations. It is important that you learn to discern when those messages can be shared with others and when they should not be shared.

"All messages from us, and from other beings of the light realms, contain keys of wisdom for your advancement and need to be integrated as you continue on your pathway to self-realization. It is more important to integrate fully what you have already received than to keep looking for the next message. Unless you integrate in your consciousness what you have already received, it becomes clutter in your mind and does not always serve you.

"The Heart of Lemuria resides in each one of you. It is our sacred mission, along with the teachings of Aurelia Louise Jones and those who work alongside her, to help you reawaken to the totality of your divinity and the sacredness of your own journey.

"Your willingness to open to energies that stretch your understanding should never be threatened by feelings of insecurity. Therefore, we continue to remind you to allow what you hear and what you read be the truth within your own heart where your authenticity resides. Only with your heart will you discern the vibrations of the Divine and determine which is appropriate for you in the now moment.

"Never hesitate to ask us for guidance in your heart. We will always answer.

"I am Adama, teacher for humanity."

A Note about Aurelia Louise Jones

On July 12th, 2009, Aurelia Louise Jones made her transition, leaving us a rich legacy of transformational tools, inspiring us to live from our hearts and fully embrace the Lemurian way of life. Through her channeling of Adama and the Masters of Light, Aurelia's teachings bring forth invaluable "food for thought" which is timeless in its nature. There has never been a more appropriate time than the present moment to attune our hearts to Love, Compassion and above all, Ascension. These are the key elements in Aurelia's heartfelt message from Adama and our Telosian family and all the Ascended Masters of Light and Love. This will set us free, moving us into the next vibrational frequencies, the fifth dimension and beyond.

Aurelia's dream and desire was to awaken humanity during this monumental time of change, to increase the Lemurian Connection around the world and to spread the Light of Adama's message through her books about Telos and the Lemurian way of living. She had great love and a deep gratitude for the planet, beloved Mother Earth, humanity and especially the animals. Her dedication was unwavering and this mission was ever present the last 10 years of her life.

Aurelia's books have touched the lives of thousands of people all over the world. Telos communities have been created in many countries through sheer inspiration to live from the Lemurian Heart. As people embrace the Telos books, study groups are forming to support one another on their sacred spiritual journey. We are grateful to have the Telos books, the teachings and channelings of Aurelia Louise Jones awaken us to our Lemurian heritage.

Mt. Shasta Light Publishing is dedicated to continuing Aurelia's heartfelt mission, spreading the Lemurian teachings and opening our hearts to Ascension. Her work continues to be distributed throughout the world.

Mount Shasta Light Publishing Publications

The Seven Sacred Flames...$39.00

Seven Sacred Flames Prayer Booklet $7.00

Ascension Activation Booklet $7.00

Seven Sacred Flames Card Deck $16.00

Telos Book Series Card Deck $16.00

Telos – Volume 1 "Revelations of the New Lemuria"..$18.00

Telos – Volume 2 "Messages for the Enlightenment
of a Humanity in Transformation"...........................$18.00

Telos – Volume 3 "Protocols of the Fifth Dimension" .$20.00

The Effects of Recreational Drugs
on Spiritual Development...$4.00

Angelo's Message – "Angelo, the Angel Cat
Speaks to all People on this Planet Regarding
the Treatment of Animals by Humanity" $8.00

These publications can be purchased in the USA:

- Directly from us by phone or at our mailing address

- From our secure shopping cart on our web site:
  http://www.mslpublishing.com

- From Amazon.com

- Bookstores through New Leaf Book Distributing

If ordering by mail, CA residents, please include 8.25% sales tax. Also include shipping charges: Priority or Media mail, according to weight and distance.

Mount Shasta Light Publishing
P.O. Box 1509
Mount Shasta, CA 96067-1509 - USA
aurelia@mslpublishing.com
Phone: (Intl: 001) 530-926-4599
(If no answer, please leave a message)

Telos and Lemurian Connection Associations

Telos USA
www.telos-usa.org
info@telos-usa.org
Also see: Lemurian Connection
www.lemurianconnection.com

Telos World-Wide Foundation, Inc.
E-mail: telos@telosinfo.org
Web Site: www.telosinfo.org

Telos Australia
www.telos-australia.com.au
robert@telos-australia.com.au
catherine@telos-australia.com.au

Telos-France
www.telos-france.com
telosfrance@me.com

Telos Europe
www.teloseurope.eu
telos-europe@me.com

Telos Finland
www.telosfinland.fi
telosfinland@me.com

Telos Japan
www.telos-japan.org
office@telos-japan.org

Canadian Distributors:

Telos World-Wide Foundation, Inc.
7400 St. Laurent, Office 326,
Montreal, QC - H2R 2Y1 – Canada
Phone: (001 Intl.) 1-514-940-7746
E-mail: telos@telosinfo.org
Web Site: www.telosinfo.org

For Canadian Bookstores:
Quanta Books Distributing
3251 Kennedy Road, Unit 20
Toronto, Ontario, MIV-2J0 - CANADA
Phone: 1-888-436-7962 or 416-410-9411
E-mail: quantamail@quanta.ca
Web: www.quanta.ca

For distributors in other languages please check our website: www.mslpublishing.com